Contents

THREEFOLD *Love*

EMBRACING GOD, SELF, AND OTHERS

metamorphosis
PUBLISHERS

OBED OLIVARRÍA

OBED OLIVARRÍA

Unless otherwise indicated, all Bible quotations are taken from the Holy Bible, New International version, copyright © 1973, 1978 by the International Bible Society. Used by permission of Zondervan Bible Publishers.

Cover design, typeset, and inside design by Obed Olivarría.

ISBN (print edition): 979-8-9913504-4-0

ISBN (eBook edition): 979-8-9913504-5-7

Library of Congress Control Number: 2024922949

First Edition: February 2025

Metamorphosis Publishers.

Santa Ana, California.

For information contact:

http://www.obedolivarria.com

Introduction: The Essence of Threefold Love

I n the hustle and bustle of daily life, we often find ourselves yearning for deeper connections—with God, with ourselves, and with those around us. In our hearts, we recognize a universal truth: we are made to love and to be loved. However, understanding and living out this love can be complex. How do we love God fully amidst our struggles and distractions? What does it mean to love ourselves in a world that constantly demands more from us? And how can we love others sincerely when relationships can be so challenging?

The Bible gives us a profound answer. In Matthew 22:37-39, Jesus distills the essence of faith into a simple yet powerful command: *"Love the Lord your God with all your heart and with all your soul and with all your mind... Love your neighbor as yourself."* These verses reveal a truth that encompasses our entire being and existence—a threefold love that involves loving God, embracing self-love, and extending that love to others. This is not a fragmented or isolated approach to love; it's a holistic journey that shapes how we view God, ourselves, and our relationships with those around us.

By embracing this divine mandate, we embark on a transformative journey of spiritual growth and self-discovery, inviting deeper connections with both the Creator and those around us. This passage beckons us to examine the depths of our love, leading us to a holistic understanding of how interconnected our relationships truly are.

This book is about exploring what it means to live out this threefold love in practical and transformative ways. Often, we think of these aspects of love as separate tasks: loving God is part of our faith, loving ourselves might seem selfish or secondary, and loving others feels like a duty that can sometimes be overwhelming. But what if these aspects of love are deeply connected? What if understanding God's love for us is the key to unlocking how we view ourselves and, in turn, how we can genuinely love others?

Loving God wholeheartedly is our initial step in nurturing this divine connection. This love is not merely an emotion, but a commitment that encompasses our entire being. As we cultivate a vibrant relationship with God, we learn to recognize His presence in our lives, guiding our thoughts, actions, and decisions. This intimate connection empowers us to develop mindfulness and self-compassion, as we begin to see ourselves through the lens of divine love.

By aligning our hearts with God's, we gain clarity about our identity, purpose, and the innate worth bestowed upon us, which enables us to love ourselves authentically. And the call to love our neighbors as ourselves highlights the importance of interpersonal relationships and communication. It challenges us to reflect on how we interact with others and urges us to embody compassion and empathy. When we truly understand our worth in God's eyes, we are better equipped to extend that love to those around us. Our relationships flourish when we practice emotional intelligence and appreciate the diverse love languages that enrich our connections.

Forgiveness and healing are crucial aspects of this threefold love. Loving our neighbors requires us to confront the inevitable conflicts and misunderstandings that arise in relationships. Jesus' command does not come with an asterisk; it invites us to embrace forgiveness as an active choice, freeing ourselves from the burdens of resentment and anger. In doing so, we align ourselves with God's grace, allowing His love to flow through us and transform our interactions. This process of healing can lead to renewed bonds, deeper understanding, and a more profound sense of connection, both with others and with ourselves.

Throughout this journey, we will dive into three interconnected parts: **Embracing God's Love**, **Embracing Self-Love**, and **Embracing Others in Love.** These are not three unrelated teachings, but rather parts of a whole, much like the intertwined nature of the Trinity. The more we grasp God's love, the more we see our true worth and are able to extend grace and love to others.

In the first part, **Embracing God's Love**, we will delve into the source of all love—God Himself. Understanding the nature of God's love is crucial because it sets the foundation for how we see everything else. The Bible describes God's love as patient, kind, enduring, and never failing. However, many of us struggle to truly experience this love in our daily lives. In this section, we will explore what it means to love God with our whole being and how this connection with the Creator transforms our hearts and minds.

The second part, **Embracing Self-Love**, addresses a topic that many believers find challenging. The idea of self-love often brings up feelings of guilt or selfishness, but the Bible encourages us to view ourselves through the lens of God's grace. When Jesus said to love our neighbor as ourselves, He implied that self-love is necessary to love others effectively. In this section, we will explore how to see ourselves as God sees us—fearfully and wonderfully made—and how embracing self-care, forgiveness, and grace can lead to spiritual growth and a healthier perspective on life.

Finally, in **Embracing Others in Love**, we will explore how our relationship with God and understanding of self-love naturally lead to loving others. Loving others, especially in difficult circumstances, can be one of the greatest challenges we face. Yet, it is in these moments that we reflect Christ's love most powerfully. We will discuss practical ways to build loving relationships, extend grace, and serve our communities as a testimony of God's love working through us.

This journey is not about mastering love in a few easy steps. Rather, it's about embracing the ongoing process of learning to love as God loves. Whether you're just beginning your faith walk or seeking to deepen your relationship with God, this book offers insights and encouragement for living a life of love that is both transformative and fulfilling. It is a journey of what I call the divine connection of cultivating love for God, for self, and others.

As we navigate the complexities of life, let us remember the simplicity of Christ's command. In every moment, we are invited to embody the love that we receive from God, sharing it generously with ourselves and the world around us. Through this, we can truly become vessels of divine love, manifesting the transformative power of Matthew 22:37-39 in our lives.

And as we embark on this journey together, let's open our hearts to the possibility that love—true, selfless, and godly love—can reshape how we view God, ourselves, and the world around us. Let's explore how the greatest commandment is not just a rule to follow, but a way of life that leads to wholeness and joy. This is the journey of threefold love: to love God fully, embrace ourselves as He created us, and love others with the same grace and compassion that we have received.

PART 1:

EMBRACING GOD'S LOVE

Chapter One

Understanding God's Unconditional Love

I remember one particular evening after a tough day at work. Everything that could go wrong did, and by the time I got home, I was questioning everything. 'Am I even doing enough? Is God even proud of me?' I sat outside in the backyard, feeling defeated. Then, something simple but profound happened. A hummingbird appeared in front of me, hovering in the quiet of the evening, its tiny wings moving impossibly fast. In that moment, I felt a strange peace. It was like God was reminding me, 'Just as you don't expect this hummingbird to do anything but be itself, I don't expect anything more from you than to simply be my child.' It was a small reminder that God's love isn't conditional on what I do—it's unconditional, just like that little bird's flight, freely given, no matter wh at.

When we hear the phrase "God loves you," it can sound so simple, almost like a cliché. Yet, behind those words lies a truth so profound that it has the power to transform lives. God's love is unlike any other love we have known; it is not based on conditions, merits, or performance. It is steadfast, unchanging, and all-encompassing. This chapter is an invitation to explore what God's unconditional love truly means and how embracing it can change our hearts and our approach to loving others.

The Nature of God's Love

The Bible is filled with descriptions of God's love, each revealing a different facet of its beauty and depth. At its core, God's love is sacrificial. In John 3:16, one of the most well-known verses in Scripture, we read, *"For God so loved the world that He gave His one and only Son, that whoever believes in Him shall not perish, but have eternal life."* This verse captures the essence of divine love: a love so vast that God Himself took on human form to rescue humanity. God's love is not mere sentiment; it is action, sacrifice, and a pursuit of relationship.

John 3:16 stands as a cornerstone of Christian belief, encapsulating the essence of God's love for humanity. This verse proclaims that God's love is not only vast and unconditional, but also deeply personal. It reminds us that love is the very foundation of our relationship with God, ourselves, and others. As we nurture our faith, we must recognize that this divine love is the source from which all other forms of love flow. Embracing this truth allows us to cultivate an atmosphere of acceptance, compassion, and understanding in our lives.

In our journey of spiritual growth and self-discovery, John 3:16 invites us to reflect on our identity as beloved children of God. This affirmation encourages us to embrace self-love and acknowledge our worthiness. When we recognize that we are cherished by the Creator, we can begin to heal the wounds of self-doubt and insecurity. This transformative process empowers us to communicate our needs and feelings more openly, fostering healthier interpersonal relationships. By embodying the love described in this verse, we learn to extend grace to ourselves and others, creating a cycle of compassion that enriches our connections.

This verse challenges us to look beyond our individual experiences and embrace the call to love others. This verse compels us to cultivate mindfulness in our interactions, seeing each person as a reflection of God's love. As we practice empathy and understanding, we develop emotional intelligence that enhances our relationships. By actively listening and affirming the experiences of those around us, we embody the spirit of love that God has shown us.

As we integrate the truths of John 3:16 into our daily lives, we find that our love for God deepens, enriching our spiritual practices and enhancing our overall well-being. This verse invites us into a dynamic relationship with the divine, where love becomes the lens through which we perceive ourselves and the world. By embracing God's love, we cultivate an environment where self-compassion flourishes, and we are empowered to build community. In doing so, we fulfill our calling to reflect God's love in every aspect of our lives, creating a legacy of love that resonates through our actions and words.

Another key aspect of God's love is that it is patient and forgiving. In the realm of forgiveness and healing, John 3:16 serves as a powerful reminder of the grace we have received. Just as God has forgiven us, we are called to extend that forgiveness to others, releasing the burdens that weigh down our hearts. This act of love is not a sign of weakness, but rather a profound strength that reflects our commitment to spiritual well-being. By letting go of grudges and embracing reconciliation, we align ourselves with God's purpose, allowing His love to flow through us and transform our relationships.

In 1 Corinthians 13:4-7, the famous "love chapter," Paul describes the characteristics of love: "*Love is patient, love is kind... It keeps no record of wrongs.*" While this passage is often used to describe how we should love others, it also reflects God's love toward us. His love is not quick to anger or easily frustrated. It is patient and enduring, giving us grace even when we fall short.

God's love is also unchanging. Unlike human love, which can fluctuate based on feelings or circumstances, God's love remains constant. Romans 8:38-39 assures us of this truth: "*For I am convinced that neither death nor life, neither angels nor demons, neither the present nor the future... will be able to separate us from the love of God that is in Christ Jesus our Lord.*" This is a powerful promise that reminds us that God's love is not dependent on anything we do. It is rooted in His character and extends to us in every situation.

In Romans 8:38-39, the Apostle Paul offers a profound assurance of the unbreakable connection we share with God's love. He boldly proclaims that nothing in all creation can separate us from this divine love, a promise that resonates deeply as we navigate our spiritual journeys. For Christians striving to embrace a threefold love—toward God, self, and others—these verses serve as a powerful reminder that our worth and identity are firmly rooted in God's unwavering affection. This knowledge nurtures our spiritual growth and self-discovery, encouraging us to explore the depths of our relationship with the Creator and to understand that we are never alone in our struggles.

As we contemplate the implications of being inseparable from God's love, we are invited to reflect on how this truth shapes our relationship with ourselves. The message of Romans 8:38-39 encourages us to practice self-compassion and mindfulness, recognizing that our flaws and imperfections do not diminish our value in the eyes of God. Instead, they provide opportunities for growth and healing. By embracing our true identity as loved children of God, we can cultivate a healthier self-image, allowing us to approach life with grace and understanding. This internal transformation empowers us to be more authentic in our interactions with others, fostering deeper connections and enriching our relationships.

As we navigate the complexities of life, let us hold fast to the truth that nothing can separate us from the love of God. This assurance propels us forward, encouraging us to cultivate a life characterized by love, compassion, and a commitment to fostering meaningful connections in our families, communities, and beyond.

While understanding the nature of God's love is crucial, it is another thing entirely to experience it personally. Many people struggle with fully accepting God's love, often feeling unworthy or believing that they must earn His favor through good deeds. Yet, the Bible teaches us that God's love is a gift, not a reward. Ephesians 2:8-9 says, *"For it is by grace you have been saved, through faith—and this is not from yourselves, it is the gift of God—not by works, so that no one can boast."*

To experience God's love, we must first approach Him humbly, with open hearts, recognizing that we are loved not because of what we do, but because of Who He is. This is a radical departure from how love is often portrayed in the world. In human relationships, love is frequently conditional: based on performance, appearance, or mutual benefit. But God's love transcends these conditions. It is offered freely, even when we feel unworthy.

When feelings of doubt or unworthiness creep in, turning to Scripture can ground us in the truth of God's love. 1 John 4:16 says, *"And so we know and rely on the love God has for us. God is love."* This verse helps to remind us that His love is not based on our feelings or circumstances; it is an intrinsic part of His nature.

How God's Love Transforms Us

Accepting God's love is not a passive experience; it is transformative. When we truly grasp how deeply we are loved by God, it changes how we see ourselves and others. God's love gives us a new identity. No longer do we need to strive for approval or validation from the world, because we are already loved and accepted by the Creator of the universe. This truth brings a sense of peace and security that cannot be shaken by external circumstances.

Experiencing God's love compels us to love others. 1 John 4:19 says, *"We love because He first loved us."* God's love fills our hearts and overflows, enabling us to extend grace, patience, and forgiveness to others. When we understand how much we have been forgiven and loved by God, we become more willing to offer the same to those around us.

This does not mean that loving others is always easy, but it becomes possible because of the love that God has poured into our hearts.

God's love also transforms our relationship with ourselves. Many people struggle with self-worth and identity, often feeling defined by their mistakes, failures, or the opinions of others. However, when we begin to see ourselves as God sees us—beloved, chosen, and precious—it changes our self-perception. We are no longer defined by our past or our shortcomings, but by the love that God has for us. This understanding is the foundation for embracing self-love, which we will explore in the next part of this book.

Living in the light of God's love is a daily choice. It involves reminding ourselves of His truths, even when our feelings or circumstances try to tell us otherwise. It means taking the time to connect with God in prayer, to rest in His presence, and to seek His guidance. It is through this ongoing relationship with God that we begin to experience His love more fully.

God's love is not just a concept to be understood; it is a reality to be lived. In moments of joy, His love gives us reason to celebrate. In times of sorrow, His love offers comfort and hope. In seasons of uncertainty, His love provides a firm foundation on which we can stand. This is the beauty of God's unconditional love—it meets us where we are, fills us with peace, and transforms us from the inside out.

As we move forward in this journey, let us keep these foundational truths in mind: first, God's love is the source of all other love, and second, God's love is transformational. By embracing His love for us, we lay the groundwork for loving ourselves and others in ways that are authentic, life-giving, and reflective of His grace. The more we understand and experience God's love, the more we will be able to live out the commandment to love Him with all our heart, soul, and mind.

In the next chapter, we will explore what it means to love God with our whole being, and how this devotion can shape every aspect of our lives. For now, may you take a moment to rest in the truth that you are deeply and unconditionally loved by God, just as you are.

Chapter Two

Loving God with Your Whole Being

O ne day, I was in full 'go-go-go' mode. I had a million things on my to-do list, and every hour seemed to fill up before I could catch my breath. By the time the evening came, I hadn't prayed, I hadn't spent any time with God, and I felt the weight of the world on my shoulders. But something inside told me to stop. So, I went into my room, shut the door, took my shoes off, and just sat on the edge of my bed. No grand prayers, no deep theological thoughts—just me and God. I opened my heart in silence. Ten minutes later, I felt lighter, like a weight had been lifted. It wasn't about the time; it was about the focus. I realized that loving God with your whole being isn't just about grand gestures; sometimes, it's about giving Him the small moments we think we don't have.

Loving God fully is the foundation of a vibrant Christian life. It is the first and greatest commandment, encompassing every part of our existence—heart, soul, and mind. In Matthew 22:37, Jesus said, *"Love the Lord your God with all your heart and with all your soul and with all your mind."* This command is both profound and challenging. It calls us to a wholehearted devotion that goes beyond mere religious practices and extends into every area of our lives. In this chapter, we will explore what it means to love God with our whole being and how this devotion can shape our daily walk with Him.

Loving God with Your Heart: A Deep and Personal Relationship

To love God with all our heart is to have a relationship with Him that is both intimate and authentic. The heart, in biblical terms, is the center of our emotions, desires, and affections. It is the part of us that forms attachments and drives our passions. When we are called to love God with all our heart, it means that our deepest desires and affections are to be directed toward Him.

This kind of love requires humility, vulnerability, and openness. God desires a relationship where we can be honest about our struggles, joys, fears, and hopes. In Psalm 62:8, David invites us to *"pour out your hearts to Him, for God is our refuge."* Loving God with our heart means allowing Him into every corner of our lives, not just the parts that seem "holy" or "worthy." It is in this honesty that intimacy with God grows.

However, loving God with our heart also means guarding it against anything that might pull us away from Him. Proverbs 4:23 advises, *"Above all else, guard your heart, for everything you do flows from it."* This involves being mindful of the things we allow into our lives—whether they are influences, habits, or desires—that can capture our affections and lead us astray. When we prioritize God as the object of our greatest love, our hearts become aligned with His, and we start to desire what He desires.

Loving God with Your Soul: The Core of Your Identity

The soul is not a separate spiritual part of a person, but rather, their entire identity and existence. That is to say, the soul is a person's entire being, a combination of their body and God's breath of life. The soul represents the core of our being—our true full identity. And loving God with our soul means that our entire sense of self is rooted in our relationship with Him. It is about finding our ultimate purpose and meaning in God, rather than in worldly achievements, status, possessions, or anything else.

In Deuteronomy 6:5, we are called to *"Love the Lord your God with all your heart and with all your soul and with all your strength."* This was a foundational command for the Israelites, reminding them that their very existence was tied to their relationship with God. Similarly, our love for God should influence the decisions we make, the values we hold, and the way we live. It involves a willingness to submit our will to God's will, trusting that His plans are better than our own.

Loving God with our soul also means seeking to become more like Him. The process of spiritual growth is about aligning our inner character with God's nature. This includes developing qualities like humility, patience, kindness, and forgiveness—characteristics that reflect God's love and holiness. As we love God with our soul, our inner life begins to mirror His goodness, and we are transformed more into His likeness.

This commandment in Deuteronomy 6:5 is not merely a directive; it is an invitation to engage deeply with the Creator, to allow love to permeate every aspect of our being. Loving God with our entire selves means that our emotions, thoughts, and actions are intertwined in a harmonious expression of devotion. As we embrace this holistic love, we find ourselves transformed, drawing closer to the heart of God and experiencing His presence in our daily lives.

Loving God with Your Mind: Pursuing God with Thoughtfulness

Often, we think of love as purely emotional, but Jesus' command also includes loving God with all our mind. This involves engaging our intellect and thoughts in our relationship with Him. God has given us the ability to think, reason, and learn, and loving Him with our mind means using these abilities to seek a deeper understanding of Who He is.

In Romans 12:2, Paul urges believers, *"Do not conform to the pattern of this world, but be transformed by the renewing of your mind."* Our minds are constantly shaped by the information and influences we encounter. By immersing ourselves in God's Word and allowing His truth to fill our thoughts, we renew our minds and align them with His perspective. This renewal enables us to discern His will and develop a mindset that reflects His love and wisdom.

Loving God with our mind also involves wrestling with questions of faith, seeking knowledge, and exploring the vastness of God's creation. The more we learn about God—through studying Scripture, theology, and the wonders of the natural world—the more our love for Him grows. This intellectual pursuit does not diminish our faith; rather, it enriches it by deepening our understanding of God's character and His plans for the world.

Mindfulness and self-compassion play essential roles in our ability to live out Deuteronomy 6:5. By being present in the moment and attentive to our inner dialogue, we can recognize how our thoughts and feelings impact our capacity to love God and others. Practicing thoughtful self-compassion allows us to navigate our struggles without judgment, fostering a nurturing environment where we can grow spiritually. As we become more attuned to our own needs, thoughts, and emotions, we can better respond to the needs of those around us, creating a atmosphere of genuine connection and support.

Loving God with our mind means taking every thought captive and making it obedient to Christ (2 Corinthians 10:5). Our thoughts can often become a battleground, filled with doubts, fears, or lies about ourselves and others. By intentionally focusing our thoughts on God's truth, we cultivate a mindset that honors Him. This involves practicing gratitude, meditating on His promises, and replacing negative or destructive thoughts with the truth of His Word.

Cultivating a Holistic Love for God

Loving God with our heart, soul, and mind is not about compartmentalizing our love into different areas. It is a holistic approach to loving God with our entire being. Each aspect—heart, soul, and mind—is interconnected and reinforces the others. When we love God with our heart, our emotions and desires are directed toward Him. When we love Him with our soul, our identity, purpose, and will are anchored in Him. When we love Him with our mind, our thoughts and understanding align with His truth.

Cultivating this holistic love for God requires intentionality and effort. It is a daily choice to prioritize our relationship with Him, to seek His presence, and to live in obedience to His commands. It involves making room in our lives for spiritual practices that nurture our love for Him.

As we grow in our love for God, it naturally overflows into other areas of our lives. Our love for Him influences how we see ourselves and how we interact with others. It changes the way we approach our work, our relationships, and our daily decisions. Loving God fully is not just about the "spiritual" parts of our lives; it encompasses every aspect of who we are.

Loving God this way shapes our identity. When we commit to loving God wholeheartedly, we begin to see ourselves through His eyes. This divine perspective fosters self-acceptance and cultivates a sense of worthiness that is not contingent on external validation. Embracing our identity as beloved creations enables us to nurture a compassionate relationship with ourselves, a practice that is essential for personal well-being. By acknowledging our imperfections and embracing God's grace, we empower ourselves to grow and evolve in our faith.

As we deepen our love for God, we are naturally inclined to extend that love to others, reinforcing the interconnectedness of our relationships. The call to love our neighbors as ourselves becomes a tangible expression of the love we receive from the Divine. This threefold love encourages us to engage in authentic communication and to foster understanding and empathy in our interpersonal relationships. When we prioritize love as the guiding principle in our interactions, we create a supportive community that reflects the heart of God, where forgiveness and healing can flourish.

Integrating the teachings of loving God with all of our beings into our daily lives not only enriches our personal faith journey, but also strengthens our communities. When we collectively embody the call to love God, ourselves, and one another, we create a powerful witness to the transformative nature of divine love. This commitment to love this way fosters an environment where emotional intelligence thrives, allowing us to engage with one another in meaningful ways. As we strive to balance our personal and spiritual well-being, we become beacons of hope and healing, inspiring others to embark on their own journeys of love and connection.

Thirsting For God

In Psalm 63:1, David invites us into a deep, intimate space of connection with God, where our souls can thirst for His presence as parched land longs for rain. The verse says, "*You, God, are my God, earnestly I seek you. I thirst for you; my whole being longs for you, in a dry and parched land where there is no water.*" This longing illustrated in the psalm encapsulates the essence of a heartfelt relationship with the Divine. When we acknowledge our need for God, we step into a transformative journey that not only nurtures our spirit, but also enhances our capacity to love ourselves and others. This verse serves as a powerful reminder that our spiritual growth begins with recognizing our yearning for something greater than ourselves, igniting a flame of devotion that can illuminate our paths.

In the hustle and bustle of daily life, it is easy to overlook this profound thirst. Yet, this verse calls us to mindfulness, urging us to pause and reflect on our spiritual needs. By cultivating a practice of awareness, we can open our hearts to the gentle whispers of God, finding solace in moments of prayer and meditation. This intentional focus on our connection with the Divine fosters self-compassion, allowing us to embrace our imperfections and acknowledge our struggles. As we learn to love ourselves through the lens of God's grace, we become empowered to extend that same love to others, enriching our interpersonal relationships.

The essence of this psalm also teaches us about the importance of vulnerability in our relationships. Just as David expressed his longing for God, we too can communicate our needs and desires within our faith-based communities. By sharing our spiritual journeys, we cultivate deeper connections with those around us, fostering an environment of support and encouragement. This openness not only strengthens our bonds, but also enhances our emotional intelligence, allowing us to navigate the complexities of human relationships with empathy and understanding. When we embrace our vulnerabilities, we create spaces for healing and forgiveness, essential components in nurturing lasting b onds.

Psalm 63:1 invites us to explore the depths of our faith, encouraging us to seek God earnestly and wholeheartedly. Thirst for God! By prioritizing our relationship with God, we cultivate resilience that spills over into every aspect of our lives. And as we develop this divine connection, we begin to witness the transformation within ourselves and our relationships. Our capacity for love expands, allowing us to engage with the world in more meaningful ways. By embracing this sacred longing and integrating spiritual practices into our daily lives, we not only deepen our relationship with God, but also foster a harmonious existence that celebrates love in all its forms.

Responding to God's Love with Devotion

Our love for God is a response to the love He has already shown us. 1 John 4:19 reminds us, "*We love because He first loved us.*" Understanding that our love is a response liberates us from the pressure to earn God's love. Instead, we are invited to enter into a relationship with the One Who loved us before we even knew Him.

As we reflect on what it means to love God with all our heart, soul, and mind, let us commit to nurturing this love daily. Let us seek to know God more deeply, to open our hearts to His presence, and to allow His truth to renew our minds. This journey of loving God is not a destination to be reached, but a lifelong pursuit that continually shapes and transforms us.

In the next chapter, we will explore how experiencing God's presence in our lives can further deepen our love for Him and empower us to live out His love in practical ways. For now, may we take a moment to invite God into every part of our being and to express our love for Him, knowing that He delights in our devotion.

Chapter Three

Experiencing God's Presence

O ne afternoon, as usual, I was stuck in horrible traffic coming from work. It had already been a very stressful day, and now I was stuck, bumper to bumper, staring at the taillights of the car in front of me. I could feel frustration bubbling up—there were a million things I still needed to do. There was work stuff, church stuff, family stuff, and personal things. But then, something shifted. I turned the radio off and let the silence fill the car. In that quiet, I felt God's presence, soft but undeniable. It was like He was saying, 'I'm here, even in this traffic jam.' Suddenly, the frustration melted away. It was a small moment, but it reminded me that God's presence isn't limited to the pews of a church or quiet times of prayer; He's there in the everyday chaos, too.

Loving God fully is not just about acknowledging His existence or following a set of rules. It's about encountering His presence in our everyday lives. God's presence is the heartbeat of our relationship with Him, offering peace, guidance, and strength for each moment we face. In this chapter, we'll explore how to experience God's presence, the transformative power it brings, and how it shapes our journey of love.

Seeking God's Presence in Daily Life

Experiencing God's presence doesn't require a dramatic event or spiritual milestone. God is with us in every moment, whether extraordinary or mundane. Psalm 139:7-10 paints a beautiful picture of this reality: "*Where can I go from your Spirit? Where can I flee from your presence? If I go up to the heavens, you are there; if I make my bed in the depths, you are there."* God's presence is everywhere, yet we often become so preoccupied with the busyness of life that we overlook it.

To encounter God's presence daily, we must first cultivate a posture of seeking Him. Jeremiah 29:13 says, *"You will seek Me and find Me when you seek Me with all your heart."* This promise reminds us that God is not distant or hiding; He desires to reveal Himself to us. Our role is to intentionally seek Him amidst the distractions and noise of our everyday lives.

One of the most effective ways to do this is through prayer. Prayer is more than simply talking to God; it is an invitation for God to enter into our circumstances and for us to become aware of His presence. It is in prayer that we quiet our hearts, lay down our burdens, and open ourselves to listen to God's voice. Jesus modeled this practice throughout His ministry, often retreating to quiet places to pray and connect with the Father (Luke 5:16). In following His example, we create space for God to speak, comfort, and guide us.

Another way to experience God's presence is by spending time in His Word. The Bible is a living, active revelation of God's character and will. Hebrews 4:12 describes it as *"alive and active, sharper than any double-edged sword."* When we read Scripture with a heart open to hear from God, we encounter His presence through the truths and promises found within its pages. Whether it's through daily devotional reading, meditating on a single verse, or studying a specific passage, immersing ourselves in God's Word brings us into a deeper awareness of Who He is.

God's Presence in Solitude and Community

Experiencing God's presence often involves both solitude and community. Solitude allows us to withdraw from the distractions of life and be alone with God. It is in these quiet moments that we can hear His still, small voice. Psalm 46:10 encourages us, *"Be still, and know that I am God."* In stillness, we acknowledge God's sovereignty and give Him room to speak to our hearts.

Creating times of solitude can be challenging in our fast-paced world, but it is essential for nurturing our relationship with God. This might mean setting aside a specific time each day for prayer and reflection or taking a few moments throughout the day to pause and acknowledge God's presence. During these times, we can pour out our hearts to God, listen for His guidance, and simply rest in His love.

However, God also reveals His presence through the community of believers. Jesus promised in Matthew 18:20, *"For where two or three gather in my name, there am I with them."* When we join with others in worship, prayer, and fellowship, we experience God's presence in a unique and powerful way. The church, as the body of Christ, becomes a place where we can encounter God's love through the encouragement, support, and prayers of others.

God often uses community to speak into our lives, provide comfort, and remind us of His truths. Being part of a large or small group, Bible study, or regular fellowship with other believers can significantly impact our spiritual growth and help us remain aware of God's presence. It is through these relationships that we practice and experience the love of God in tangible ways.

The Transformative Power of God's Presence

Experiencing God's presence transforms us. When we spend time with God, we begin to see the world and ourselves through His eyes. In His presence, our fears are calmed, our burdens are lifted, and our hearts are renewed. This is because God's presence is not passive; it is active and life-changing.

Moses' encounter with God on Mount Sinai is a striking example of how God's presence can transform a person. After spending time in God's presence, Moses' face shone so brightly that he had to cover it with a veil (Exodus 34:29-35). While our encounters with God may not be as visibly dramatic, they do leave an imprint on our hearts. As we spend time with God, we become more like Him—more loving, patient, kind, and forgiving.

God's presence also provides strength and guidance for our daily walk. In Isaiah 41:10, God promises, *"Do not fear, for I am with you; do not be dismayed, for I am your God. I will strengthen you and help you; I will uphold you with my righteous right hand."* When we are conscious of God's presence, we face life's challenges with a different perspective. We know that we are not alone, and we have the assurance that God is with us, helping us navigate each situation.

In the context of the threefold love—embracing God, self, and others—Isaiah 41:10 invites us to confront our fears and anxieties. When we acknowledge God's unwavering presence, we can begin to dismantle the barriers that prevent us from fully loving ourselves and extending that love to others. By recognizing that we are upheld by a higher power, we cultivate a sense of security that fosters self-compassion. This self-love is essential in our ability to engage honestly and openly with others, enriching our interpersonal relationships.

Mindfulness plays a crucial role in responding to the divine assurance found in this verse. By practicing mindfulness, we can become more attuned to our thoughts and emotions, allowing us to recognize when fear or doubt arises. Isaiah 41:10 encourages us to replace these feelings with trust in God's support, creating a space where love can flourish. Mindfulness enables us to appreciate our spiritual journey while also grounding us in the present moment, ensuring that we do not become overwhelmed by past regrets or future uncertainties. When we accept God's promise to strengthen and uphold us, we become empowered to extend that same support to those around us. This dynamic fosters a faith-based community where individuals uplift one another, embodying the love languages that resonate within each person.

Moreover, God's presence also brings peace that transcends our circumstances. Philippians 4:7 describes it as *"the peace of God, which transcends all understanding, [that] will guard your hearts and your minds in Christ Jesus."* This peace is not dependent on the absence of trouble, but rather, on the presence of God. When we focus on God instead than on our circumstances, we experience a sense of calm and confidence that comes from knowing He is in control.

Inviting God's Presence into Every Moment

Experiencing God's presence is not limited to specific times of prayer or worship. We can invite God into every moment of our lives—whether we're at school, work, driving, playing, working out, spending time with family, or resting. Brother Lawrence, a 17th-century monk, wrote about "practicing the presence of God," which involves maintaining an ongoing awareness of God throughout the day. This practice is not about adding another task to our to-do list; it's about learning to turn our thoughts and hearts toward God in the midst of our daily routines.

A simple way to begin practicing God's presence is through short prayers or acknowledgments of God throughout the day. When facing a difficult situation, we can whisper a quick prayer: "Lord, I know You are with me." When experiencing joy or success, we can pause to thank God for His blessings. These small acts of turning our hearts toward God help us become more aware of His presence and remind us that He is involved in every aspect of our lives.

Psalm 16:11 beautifully encapsulates the profound connection we share with God, as it proclaims, "*You make known to me the path of life; in your presence there is fullness of joy; at your right hand are pleasures forevermore.*" This verse invites us to explore the divine relationship that fosters love for God, self, and others. In our spiritual journey, recognizing that true fulfillment comes from God's presence transforms how we perceive life's challenges and joys. Embracing this truth helps us cultivate a deeper love for ourselves and others, as we learn that our worth is rooted in our connection with the Divine.

The essence of this psalm emphasizes the importance of seeking God's guidance and welcoming His presence in our daily lives. When we acknowledge that God illuminates our paths, we open ourselves to a journey of self-discovery and spiritual growth. This awareness encourages us to reflect on our thoughts and actions, helping us to align them with our divine purpose. As we navigate our own lives, we can extend this understanding to our relationships, recognizing that when we seek God's wisdom and company, we become better equipped to love and communicate with those around us. This pursuit of divine guidance fosters an environment of compassion that strengthens our interpersonal connections.

Psalm 16:11 also reminds us that joy and pleasure are found in the company of God, and this sentiment extends to our relationships with one another. Building a community rooted in God's love allows us to practice forgiveness and healing, creating a safe space for vulnerability and growth. Together, we can celebrate the divine presence that unites us and inspires us to love more deeply.

Finding joy in God's presence transforms our perspective, enabling us to approach challenges with a renewed sense of hope and purpose. As we cultivate this divine connection, we are empowered to love ourselves and others authentically. The journey of self-discovery, grounded in faith, leads us to a life marked by compassion, joy, and a profound sense of belonging. Embracing God's guiding not only enriches our own lives, but also radiates love to those around us, creating a ripple effect of grace and connection in our communities.

Resting in God's Presence

Resting in God's presence means letting go of our anxieties, fears, and need for control, and trusting that God is enough. It is the realization that we do not have to strive for God's love; we are already loved. In His presence, we find rest for our souls, as Jesus invites us in Matthew 11:28: "*Come to me, all you who are weary and burdened, and I will give you rest.*"

As we rest in God's presence, we are filled with His love, which overflows into how we love ourselves and others. This rest is not about inactivity; it is about living from a place of security in God's love and grace. It is knowing that we are held by the One Who loves us unconditionally.

In the next part of this book, we will explore how this experience of God's love enables us to embrace self-love—not in a self-centered way, but in a manner that reflects God's view of who we are. For now, may we commit to seeking God's presence daily and inviting Him into every moment of our lives, knowing that His presence brings transformation, peace, and strength.

PART 2:

EMBRACING SELF-LOVE

Chapter Four

Seeing Yourself Through God's Eyes

When I was about to graduate college, I went through a rough patch where I felt like I wasn't enough. My grades were great, but for personal reasons, I just didn't feel like I measured up. Everyone around me seemed to be doing better, accomplishing more or getting desired jobs waiting for them after graduation. I didn't, and it didn't feel good. One evening, after venting to a close friend, he said something that stopped me in my tracks: 'You know, you're already enough for God, right? None of this other stuff matters to Him.' It was such a simple statement, but it hit me like a ton of bricks. I had been so focused on trying to prove myself to the world that I forgot God had already declared my worth long before. It was the reminder I needed—that I am fearfully and wonderfully made, just as I am.

The concept of self-love can feel complicated, particularly within the Christian faith. Many of us have been taught to put others before ourselves, to serve selflessly, and to live humbly. While these teachings are certainly biblical, they can sometimes lead to a misunderstanding: that loving oneself is inherently selfish, narcissistic, or wrong. However, Jesus' command to *"love your neighbor as yourself"* (Matthew 22:39) implies that self-love is not only permissible, but also essential. After all, how can we genuinely love others if we do not understand or accept the love that God has for us?

To love ourselves in a healthy, God-honoring way, we must first learn to see ourselves as God sees us. Our worth is not derived from our achievements, education, income, appearance, or status; it is rooted in who we are in Christ. This chapter will explore the biblical perspective of self-worth, the importance of self-compassion, and how embracing our identity in Christ is foundational for loving ourselves well.

Our Identity in Christ: Wonderfully Made and Deeply Loved

The Bible is clear about our value in God's eyes. In Psalm 139:14, the psalmist declares, "*I praise you because I am fearfully and wonderfully made; your works are wonderful, I know that full well.*" This verse is not just poetic sentiment; it is a profound truth. We are God's creation, crafted with care and intention. Every aspect of our being—our physical features, personalities, gifts, and even our quirks—is part of God's wonderful design.

However, it can be challenging to believe this when we live in a world that constantly tells us we are not enough. Society bombards us with messages that our worth is tied to how we look, what we achieve, or how we compare to others. These voices can drown out the truth of who we are in God's eyes. When we internalize these messages, we begin to view ourselves through a distorted lens, leading to self-criticism, insecurity, and shame.

This is why it is crucial to root our identity in what God says about us, not in what the world dictates. In Ephesians 2:10, Paul writes, "*For we are God's handiwork, created in Christ Jesus to do good works, which God prepared in advance for us to do.*" This verse affirms that we are not random products of chance, but purposeful creations. We are "handiwork"—masterpieces crafted by the Creator Himself. When we see ourselves as God's masterpiece, we start to recognize our inherent worth, regardless of our shortcomings or failures.

Ephesians 2:10 encapsulates the essence of who we are as individuals in the divine narrative. Each person is uniquely crafted, not merely to exist but to thrive in a purpose that resonates deeply with God's love. Embracing this truth allows us to see ourselves through the lens of divine intention, fostering a sense of value and purpose that transcends the mundane aspects of life. As we cultivate love for God, self, and others, we begin to understand that our existence is part of a larger tapestry woven by the Creator.

In our spiritual growth and self-discovery, acknowledging this truth can ignite a transformative journey. Recognizing ourselves as God's workmanship instills a sense of dignity and worth that encourages us to explore our gifts and talents. Each of us possesses unique abilities that can contribute to the world around us, and when we align our actions with God's purpose, we find fulfillment and joy. This process requires mindfulness and self-compassion, as we learn to appreciate our strengths while also accepting our weaknesses. It is through this balance that we can engage in authentic self-discovery, leading us closer to understanding our divine calling.

Interpersonal relationships are significantly enriched when we embrace our identity as God's creations. When we acknowledge that everyone we encounter is also God's hand-iwork, we foster a culture of respect and kindness. By nurturing relationships grounded in love and understanding, we create a supportive community that reflects the heart of God, promoting healing and reconciliation in our interactions.

Understanding that we are all works in progress, shaped by God's grace, allows us to extend compassion to ourselves and others. This perspective fosters an environment where forgiveness can flourish, as we recognize that everyone is on their own journey of growth and discovery. By integrating this understanding into our lives, we build a faith-based community that is resilient, loving, and supportive, embodying the threefold love we are called to embrace. Through this divine connection, we become catalysts for change, inspiring others to recognize their worth and purpose in God's grand design.

Additionally, Psalm 139:14 invites us into a profound understanding of our identity as beloved creations of God. As we reflect on these words, we are reminded that embracing our uniqueness is a crucial step in cultivating a deeper love for God, ourselves, and others. Recognizing that we are fearfully and wonderfully made encourages us to appreciate not only our individual attributes but also the divine handiwork that exists in each person we encounter. This realization can transform our relationships, fostering a spirit of compassion and acceptance within our faith-based communities.

In the journey of spiritual growth and self-discovery, Psalm 139:14 serves as a cor-nerstone for understanding our intrinsic value. When we internalize the truth that we are crafted with intention and care, we begin to shed the burdens of comparison and self-doubt. Embracing our God-given identity allows us to approach our lives with co-nfidence, empowering us to express our authentic selves without fear of judgment. This self-acceptance is not a destination, but an ongoing process that invites us to explore the depths of our hearts and the gifts we bring to the world. As we dive deeper into this journey, we discover that loving ourselves is not a selfish act, but a prerequisite for truly loving others.

When we grasp the significance of our unique designs, we begin to view others through a lens of appreciation rather than critique. This shift in perspective cultivates the spiritual maturity that allows us to engage with empathy and understanding, and helps us recog-nize the divine spark within each person, fostering a culture of respect and kindness. Our ability to celebrate diversity enriches our communities, as we learn to communicate not just with words, but with hearts that resonate with love and compassion.

At the same time, when we acknowledge our own imperfections and the grace that God extends to us, we become more equipped to extend that same grace to others. This cycle of love and forgiveness is essential for healing in relationships, allowing us to navigate conflicts with humility and understanding. As we learn to forgive ourselves and others, we create space for deeper connections, grounded in the knowledge that we are all fearfully and wonderfully made, each on our own journey of growth and transformation.

As we cultivate this divine connection, we not only become more attuned to our own needs, but also to the needs of others, creating a ripple effect of love that extends beyond ourselves. Through this journey, we can embody the essence of the threefold love, enriching our lives and the lives of those we touch.

God's love for us is not conditional. Romans 5:8 tells us, *"But God demonstrates His own love for us in this: While we were still sinners, Christ died for us."* God's love for us is not based on our performance, moral behavior, or accomplishments. It is based solely on His character and grace. Accepting this truth liberates us from the pressure to prove our worth and allows us to embrace the fact that we are already loved and valued by God.

Embracing Self-Compassion: The Biblical Mandate to Love Ourselves

Self-love is often misunderstood as self-centeredness or pride, but biblical self-love is about recognizing and accepting our worth as children of God. This includes showing ourselves the same grace and compassion that we would offer others. When Jesus said, " *Love your neighbor as yourself"* (Mark 12:31), He acknowledged that how we treat ourselves affects how we treat others. If we are harsh, critical, or unforgiving toward ourselves, it becomes difficult to genuinely extend love and grace to others.

One of the most important aspects of self-love is self-compassion. Self-compassion means acknowledging our struggles, failures, and imperfections without harsh judgment. It means being kind to ourselves when we fall short and offering ourselves the same forgiveness that God freely gives us. In 1 John 1:9, we are reminded, *"If we confess our sins, he is faithful and just and will forgive us our sins and purify us from all unrighteousness."* If God, Who is perfect and holy, extends forgiveness to us, how much more should we forgive ourselves?

Practicing self-compassion also involves recognizing that we are human and that making mistakes is a part of our growth process. We are works in progress, continually being shaped and refined by God. Philippians 1:6 encourages us with these words: " *Being confident of this, that He Who began a good work in you will carry it on to completion until the day of Christ Jesus.*" Embracing this truth allows us to approach ourselves with grace, knowing that God is patient and committed to our growth.

Self-Love in Action: Nurturing Our Whole Being

Loving ourselves as God loves us involves caring for our entire being—body, mind, and spirit. Our physical health, mental well-being, and spiritual growth are all interconnected, and neglecting one aspect affects the others. When we prioritize self-care, we honor the life that God has given us and position ourselves to love others more effectively.

1 Corinthians 6:19-20 reminds us, "Do you not know that your bodies are temples of the Holy Spirit, who is in you, whom you have received from God? You are not your own; you were bought at a price. Therefore honor God with your bodies." This passage underscores the importance of caring for our physical health. Eating well, getting enough rest, exercising, and addressing health concerns are not acts of vanity or selfishness; they are ways of honoring God by taking care of the body He has entrusted to us.

Similarly, mental and emotional self-care is vital. We live in a world filled with stress, anxiety, and pressures that can weigh heavily on our hearts and minds. Jesus Himself took time to rest and withdraw to quiet places, demonstrating the importance of caring for our inner well-being (Mark 6:31). Taking time to rest, reflect, and recharge is not a sign of weakness; it is an acknowledgment that we are finite beings who need God's strength to carry on.

Spiritual self-care, such as spending time in prayer, reading Scripture, and being in fellowship with other believers, nurtures our relationship with God and reminds us of who we are in Him. When we consistently connect with God, we are filled with His love, which overflows into how we view ourselves and others. This daily practice of drawing near to God grounds us in our identity as His beloved children.

Letting Go of Self-Criticism and Embracing God's Grace

One of the greatest obstacles to self-love is self-criticism. We often hold ourselves to impossible standards, condemning ourselves for every mistake or perceived inadequacy. While self-examination is necessary for growth, self-condemnation is not. Romans 8:1 assures us, "Therefore, there is now no condemnation for those who are in Christ Jesus." If God, who is the ultimate judge, does not condemn us, then we have no right to condemn ourselves.

Embracing self-love means letting go of the negative self-talk and unrealistic expectations that we place on ourselves. It means choosing to speak to ourselves with the same kindness and grace that we would extend to a dear friend. This shift in perspective does not ignore our faults or failures; rather, it acknowledges them and brings them to God, trusting in His forgiveness and transformative power.

Self-Love as the Foundation for Loving Others

In 1 John 4:7-8, we are reminded of the profound and transformative nature of love, encapsulated in the powerful declaration that "*God is love.*" This foundational truth invites us to explore love not merely as an emotion, but as the very essence of our Creator. We are called to embrace this divine love, allowing it to shape our understanding of ourselves and our relationships with others. This passage serves as a cornerstone for cultivating a threefold love—embracing God, self, and others—an invitation to experience spiritual growth and self-discovery that resonates deeply within our hearts.

First, to love God is to acknowledge His presence in every aspect of our lives. It is through this love that we find our identity and purpose, as we are created in His image. When we cultivate a relationship with God, we open ourselves to the fullness of love that He offers. Then, as we do this, this love then transforms our hearts, allowing us to extend empathy and compassion, as well as grace and understanding to ourselves too. In our journey of self-discovery, we learn that loving ourselves is not an act of selfishness, but a reflection of God's love within us. And as we embrace this truth, we can navigate our spiritual growth with confidence, knowing that we are worthy of love and kindness.

The call to love one another is equally significant in this passage. When we understand that love originates from God, we recognize our responsibility to embody that love in our relationships with others. This divine connection fosters a sense of community, where forgiveness and healing become possible. And in this divine connection, we discover the profound truth that love is not just what we do; it is who we are.

So, loving ourselves is not about self-indulgence or selfishness; it is about embracing the truth of who we are in Christ. When we understand that we are fearfully and wonderfully made, masterworks, loved unconditionally by God, and yet, still under construction, we become free to love others from a place of wholeness. Our self-love sets the tone for how we treat others, for it is only when we accept God's grace for ourselves that we can extend it to those around us.

In the next chapter, we will explore the practice of self-care as a divine mandate and how tending to our physical, emotional, and spiritual needs is essential for living out a life of love. For now, may we take a moment to rest in the knowledge that we are deeply loved by God, just as we are, and allow that love to shape how we see and treat ourselves.

Chapter Five

Self-Care as a Divine Mandate

I used to pride myself on being the 'go-to' person. Need something? I was there. Extra project at work? I'd take it on. Helping a friend move on short notice? Sure, why not? Church volunteering? Of course, count me in! I thrived on staying busy—until one day, I didn't. I hit a wall. Physically, emotionally, spiritually—I was burnt out. This happened recently, by the way. I clearly remember lying on the couch one Saturday afternoon, too tired to even think, when my daughter came up and asked me to play with her. I couldn't even muster the energy to say 'yes.' That's when it hit me: I had been giving so much to everyone else, that I had nothing left for the people I loved most—or for God. From that day, I started seeing self-care not as a luxury, but as a necessity, a way to stay healthy so I could continue to serve God and others. If I was to give my best, I needed to take care of m yself first.

Self-care often gets a bad rap, especially within Christian circles. It's easy to see it as selfish or self-indulgent, conflicting with the biblical call to deny oneself and serve others. Yet, when understood in its proper context, self-care is not only appropriate, but necessary. Caring for our physical, mental, and spiritual well-being is a vital part of loving ourselves as God commands. In fact, it's an act of stewardship over the life that God has entrusted to us.

In this chapter, we will explore the biblical foundation for self-care, discuss the balance between self-care and self-sacrifice, and provide practical steps for nurturing our whole being. By seeing self-care as a divine mandate, we come to understand that tending to our own well-being enables us to love God and others more effectively.

The Biblical Foundation for Self-Care

The idea of caring for oneself is not a modern invention; it has biblical roots. Jesus Himself modeled self-care during His ministry on Earth. Despite His demanding schedule of teaching, healing, and serving others, Jesus took deliberate steps to care for His physical, emotional, and spiritual needs. In Mark 6:31, He said to His disciples, "*Come with Me by yourselves to a quiet place and get some rest.*" Jesus recognized the importance of rest and solitude, not just for Himself but also for His followers. He understood that they needed time away from the demands of life to rejuvenate and reconnect with God.

This profound invitation serves as a reminder of the importance of stillness in our spiritual journeys. In the hustle and bustle of life, we often forget that true connection with God, ourselves, and others necessitates moments of retreat and reflection. By embracing these pauses, we cultivate a deeper love for God as we quiet our minds and allow His voice to resonate within us. This is a powerful step toward nurturing our spiritual growth, where we can discover the richness of God's presence in our lives.

As we consider the implications of this verse, we realize that self-care is not merely a trend; it is an essential practice rooted in our faith. The invitation to rest is a call to honor our own needs, recognizing that we cannot pour into others without first being filled ourselves. When we take time to recharge, we align with God's design for our well-being. This aligns with the concept of self-love, where acknowledging our own worth allows us to engage more authentically in our relationships with others. Thus, embracing rest becomes an act of love not only for ourselves, but also for those we encounter.

Jesus instructs His disciples to come away together, emphasizing the importance of communal rest and rejuvenation. In our faith-based communities, we are called to support one another in these moments of retreat. By sharing in each other's burdens and joys, we foster an environment of forgiveness and healing. As we cultivate connections grounded in love, we reflect the heart of Christ, inviting others to experience the grace that flows from Him through us.

Another biblical foundation for self-care is found in the concept of Sabbath. In Genesis 2:2-3, we read that God rested on the seventh day after creating the world. While God does not need rest in the human sense, He set an example for us, highlighting the importance of ceasing from our labors to recharge and reflect. The Sabbath is a reminder that our worth is not based on our productivity, and it invites us to trust in God's provision rather than our efforts. When we honor the rhythm of work and rest that God established, we practice a form of self-care that aligns with His design for our lives.

Furthermore, the Bible speaks of our bodies as temples of the Holy Spirit. In 1 Corinthians 6:19-20, Paul writes, *"Do you not know that your bodies are temples of the Holy Spirit, Who is in you, Whom you have received from God? You are not your own; you were bought at a price. Therefore honor God with your bodies."*

Here, Paul reminds us that we are not merely physical entities, but vessels filled with divine presence. Understanding this truth compels us to treat ourselves and others with honor and respect, recognizing that every interaction is an opportunity to manifest God's love. This realization also encourages us to engage in practices that nurture our spiritual and emotional well-being. We learn to listen to our thoughts and feelings with grace, allowing ourselves the space to rest, recharge, grow, and heal.

Understanding our bodies as sacred spaces directly influences our relationships with others. When we honor ourselves, we naturally extend that honor to those around us. This principle of loving our neighbor as ourselves becomes a lived reality, enriching our interpersonal connections. As we come together, united in the understanding that we are collectively the body of Christ, we are empowered to support one another in our spiritual journeys. This unity encourages us to share our struggles and triumphs openly, promoting an atmosphere of grace, forgiveness, learning, and healing. In such a community, we learn the importance of uplifting one another, creating a sanctuary where love is actively demonstrated, and everyone feels valued and accepted.

Caring for our health—mental, physical, and spiritual—is neither narcissism, vanity, nor selfishness; it is an act of honoring God. It is expected of us. And when we take care of ourselves, fully and faithfully, we acknowledge that our bodies and minds are gifts from God, meant to be used for His purposes.

Finding Balance: Self-Care and Self-Sacrifice

One of the challenges in embracing self-care as a Christian is balancing it with the biblical call to self-sacrifice. Jesus said in Matthew 16:24, *"Whoever wants to be my disciple must deny themselves and take up their cross and follow Me."* This call to deny oneself can seem at odds with the idea of self-care. However, self-care and self-sacrifice are not mutually exclusive; they are complementary aspects of a healthy spiritual life.

Self-care becomes problematic when it turns into self-centeredness, where our primary focus is on fulfilling our own desires at the expense of others. True self-care, however, is about maintaining the health of our physical, mental, and spiritual selves so that we can serve God and others effectively. It recognizes that we cannot pour from an empty cup. When we neglect our well-being, we quickly become depleted, stressed, and burnt out, which hinders our ability to love others as God commands.

Jesus' life provides a perfect example of this balance. He lived a life of radical self-sacrifice, ultimately giving His life on the cross for our sins. Yet, He also practiced self-care. He withdrew to solitary places to pray (Luke 5:16), rested when He was weary, and took time to be with close friends. By doing so, Jesus demonstrated that self-care is not about selfish indulgence; it is about nurturing our relationship with God and maintaining our well-being so we can fulfill the purposes He has for us.

Practical Steps for Self-Care

Understanding that self-care is a divine mandate is one thing, but knowing how to practice it is another. Self-care involves caring for our whole being—body and mind. Here are some practical steps to help us incorporate self-care into our daily lives in a way that honors God:

1. Prioritize Rest and Sabbath

In our fast-paced world, rest is often seen as a luxury rather than a necessity. Yet, God designed us to need rest. Make it a priority to set aside time for rest each day, but also to observe, practice, and honor the Sabbath each week. Use this time to step away from work, reflect on God's goodness, and do things that bring joy and refreshment to your soul. Remember, rest is not just physical; it also involves emotional and spiritual rest. Spend time physically resting, but also make time for prayer, worship, and solitude, allowing God to replenish your spirit.

2. Care for Your Physical Health

As we were reminded, our bodies are temples of the Holy Spirit, and caring for them is an act of worship. This includes eating nutritious food, exercising regularly, and getting enough sleep. While it can be tempting to push our physical limits to meet the demands of life, doing so neglects the stewardship of the body God has given us. Make small, manageable changes to your routine, such as taking a daily walk, drinking more water, eating less junk food, and creating a consistent sleep schedule. These simple acts of self-care can have a profound impact on your overall well-being.

3. Practice Emotional and Mental Self-Care

Our emotional and mental health are just as important as our physical health. Take time to identify and process your emotions, and don't be afraid to seek support when needed. Talk to a trusted friend, join a support group, or consider speaking with a counselor or therapist. Philippians 4:6-7 encourages us to bring our anxieties to God in prayer: *"Do not be anxious about anything, but in every situation, by prayer and petition, with thanksgiving, present your requests to God."* Journaling, creative activities, uplifting hobbies, and setting healthy boundaries are other ways to care for your mental and emotional well-being.

4. Nourish Your Spirit

Spiritual self-care is about nurturing your relationship with God. This includes spending regular time in prayer, reading Scripture, worshiping, and being in fellowship with other believers. Find what nourishes your spirit and helps you draw closer to God. Perhaps it's taking a nature walk and marveling at His creation, listening to worship music, inspirational devotionals, or practicing meditation on His Word. When our spirits are nurtured, we are better equipped to handle life's challenges and to love others from a place of fullness.

5. Set Boundaries and Learn to Say No

Setting healthy boundaries is a crucial aspect of self-care. Jesus set boundaries during His ministry, choosing times to withdraw from the crowds and even saying no to some requests (Mark 1:35-38). It is not our responsibility to meet every need or say yes to every demand. Learn to recognize your limits and say no when necessary. Setting boundaries is not a sign of weakness; it is an acknowledgment that we are finite beings who need to care for our well-being in order to serve effectively.

Self-Care as an Act of Worship

When we practice self-care, we are not just taking care of ourselves; we are honoring the One Who created us. We are acknowledging that our lives are valuable and that we are worth caring for. In doing so, we also equip ourselves to better love and serve others. Self-care is not a distraction from our spiritual lives; it is an integral part of it.

As we embrace self-care, let us do so with a heart of gratitude, recognizing it as a gift from God. May we seek balance, wisdom, and the guidance of the Holy Spirit as we care for our bodies and minds. In the next chapter, we will explore the importance of self-forgiveness and how letting go of guilt allows us to fully embrace the life that God has called us to. For now, may we take a moment to reflect on how we can incorporate self-care into our daily lives as an act of worship and stewardship.

Chapter Six

Forgiving Yourself and Letting Go

Years ago, I made a decision I wasn't proud of, and for a long time, I couldn't shake the guilt. Every time I thought about it, I would mentally replay the mistake and beat myself up. I'd ask for God's forgiveness, but I wasn't giving it to myself. One day at church, the pastor said something simple: 'God's already forgiven you. The only person holding onto this is you.' It hit me hard. I realized I was holding myself to a standard even God wasn't holding me to. It wasn't easy, but slowly, I began to let go. And in that process, I learned what grace really meant—forgiveness not just for others, but for me too.

Forgiving others is often challenging, but for many of us, forgiving ourselves can be even more difficult. We can be our harshest critics, holding onto past mistakes, regrets, and failures long after God has forgiven us. This tendency to cling to self-condemnation not only hinders our ability to love ourselves, but also affects our capacity to love others. When Jesus commanded us to *"love your neighbor as yourself"* (Matthew 22:39), He implied that a healthy love for others starts with embracing the grace and forgiveness that God extends to us.

In this chapter, we will explore the biblical foundation of self-forgiveness, discuss the impact of self-condemnation, and offer practical steps to let go of guilt and embrace God's grace. By learning to forgive ourselves, we open our hearts to the transformative power of God's love and move toward a life of greater freedom and wholeness.

The Biblical Foundation of Self-Forgiveness

Before we can embrace self-forgiveness, we must first understand the depth of God's forgiveness. The Bible is filled with assurances of God's willingness to forgive us when we confess our sins. 1 John 1:9 promises, *"If we confess our sins, He is faithful and just and will forgive us our sins and purify us from all unrighteousness."* This passage invites us into a transformative process where acknowledgment of our shortcomings leads to divine grace. Embracing this truth is essential for cultivating a genuine love for God, as it aligns us with His nature of mercy and forgiveness. In recognizing our need for His grace, we open the door to deeper intimacy and connection with our Creator.

God does not hold our sins against us when we come to Him in repentance. Instead, He removes them *"as far as the east is from the west"* (Psalm 103:12). This truth forms the foundation for self-forgiveness: if the Creator of the universe forgives us, we must learn to extend that same grace to ourselves.

Confession is often misunderstood as merely a moment of admitting fault, but it is much more than that; it is an act of vulnerability that fosters spiritual growth. When we confess, we are not only putting our failings into the light, but also redefining our relationship with ourselves. This process of self-discovery is crucial in understanding our human limitations and the beauty of God's unconditional love. Through the lens of 1 John 1:9, we learn that our imperfections do not disqualify us from love; rather, they are opportunities for healing and renewal. As we embrace this truth, we cultivate self-compassion, allowing us to treat ourselves with the same kindness that God extends to us.

As we grow in our relationship with God, we also become equipped to extend that love to others. The act of confessing and seeking forgiveness is foundational for healthy interpersonal relationships. It teaches us humility and the importance of recognizing our role in conflicts or misunderstandings. When we embody the spirit of confession and self-forgiveness, we are empowered to forgive others, understanding that we, too, are in need of grace. This cycle of confession and forgiveness fosters deeper connections within our faith-based communities, creating environments where individuals feel safe to be authentic and vulnerable.

Self-forgiveness is not about minimizing our wrongs or making excuses for our mistakes. It is about acknowledging our shortcomings, accepting God's forgiveness, and choosing to release the burden of guilt and shame. In Philippians 3:13, Paul writes, " *Forgetting what is behind and straining toward what is ahead."* This does not mean that we ignore our past, but that we refuse to let it define us or hold us back from the life God has called us to.

This journey of spiritual growth is not merely about moving forward in life, but about cultivating a deep connection with God, ourselves, and others. The act of forgetting past failures and disappointments is a vital step in embracing God's love and grace. It invites us to release burdens that weigh us down, enabling us to fully engage in the divine possibilities that await us. Each day presents a new opportunity to experience God's love and to extend that love to ourselves and those around us.

Letting go of past mistakes opens a path for self-compassion, allowing us to acknowledge our imperfections while still striving for growth. This act of self-acceptance is crucial in balancing our personal and spiritual well-being. When we embrace ourselves as God sees us—flawed yet worthy—we begin to cultivate a love that transcends our past experiences. This love empowers us to move forward with confidence, knowing that we are constantly being shaped into our best selves.

In the context of our relationships, Philippians 3:13 encourages us to practice forgiveness and healing. Relationships often carry the weight of past grievances and misunderstandings, which can hinder our ability to connect deeply with others. By choosing to forget what lies behind, we can extend grace to those who have wronged us, fostering an environment where love can flourish. This commitment to moving forward not only strengthens our interpersonal connections, but also reflects our understanding of God's unending forgiveness toward us. By being present in the moment, we can better appreciate the beauty of God's creation and the relationships we are building. It allows us to engage authentically with ourselves and others

Accepting God's forgiveness means that we are no longer defined by our sins or failures. Our identity is in Christ, Who has made us new creations (2 Corinthians 5:17). When we hold onto guilt, we deny the power of Christ's redemptive work on the cross. Self-forgiveness, then, is an act of faith in God's grace and a recognition of our identity as His beloved children.

The Impact of Self-Condemnation

Holding onto guilt and refusing to forgive ourselves can have a profound impact on our spiritual, emotional, and mental well-being. When we engage in self-condemnation, we keep ourselves trapped in a cycle of shame and regret, which can lead to feelings of unworthiness and inadequacy. This mindset not only damages our self-esteem, but also distorts our relationship with God. We begin to view ourselves as failures rather than as forgiven and redeemed by His grace.

Self-condemnation can also affect our relationships with others. When we are harsh and critical of ourselves, we may project these feelings onto those around us. We might struggle with accepting love or forgiveness from others because we don't believe we deserve it. This internal struggle can create barriers to genuine connection and intimacy in our relationships.

Moreover, self-condemnation often leads to a sense of spiritual paralysis. We become so focused on our past mistakes that we hesitate to step into the future that God has prepared for us. We might avoid serving others, doing ministry, pursuing our God-given dreams, or building meaningful relationships because we feel unworthy. This is not the life that God intends for us. Jesus said, *"I have come that they may have life, and have it to the full"* (John 10:10). A life marked by shame and self-condemnation is not a full life; it is a life burdened by chains that Christ has already broken.

Letting Go: Steps to Embrace Self-Forgiveness

Forgiving ourselves is a process that requires intentionality and the work of the Holy Spirit in our hearts. Here are some steps to help us let go of guilt and embrace the grace God has given us:

1. Acknowledge Your Mistakes Honestly

The first step to self-forgiveness is to honestly acknowledge our mistakes, sins, and regrets. This means facing the truth about our actions without trying to justify or excuse them. It is important to remember that self-forgiveness is not about pretending that we did nothing wrong; it is about recognizing our mistakes and bringing them to God. Psalm 51:3-4 illustrates David's acknowledgment of his sin: *"For I know my transgressions, and my sin is always before me. Against You, You only, have I sinned."* Being honest with ourselves and with God is the starting point for healing.

2. Receive God's Forgiveness

Once we have acknowledged our mistakes, we need to bring them to God and receive His forgiveness. This involves confessing our sins, repenting, and trusting in the promise of His grace. As we confess, we can be assured that God is faithful and just to forgive us (1 John 1:9). Let the truth of God's forgiveness wash over you, remembering that His grace is greater than any of your failures. This step is about moving from knowledge to belief—believing that you are truly forgiven and cleansed by God.

3. Release the Burden of Guilt

Guilt serves a purpose in leading us to repentance, but once we have repented, it no longer has a place in our lives. Continuing to carry guilt after God has forgiven us is like picking up a burden that God has already carried for you and completely removed. Jesus invites us to lay our burdens at His feet: "*Come to Me, all you who are weary and burdened, and I will give you rest*" (Matthew 11:28). Let go of the guilt and trust that God's grace is sufficient for you. If the enemy tries to remind you of your past, stand firm in the truth that you are forgiven and free in Christ.

4. Speak Truth Over Yourself

Negative self-talk is a common barrier to self-forgiveness. We often replay our mistakes in our minds, telling ourselves that we are failures, unworthy, or beyond redemption. To combat this, we must replace these lies with the truth of God's Word. Speak scriptures over yourself, such as Romans 8:1: "*Therefore, there is now no condemnation for those who are in Christ Jesus.*" Remind yourself that you are a new creation (2 Corinthians 5:17) and that God has a future and a hope for you (Jeremiah 29:11). By speaking God's truth, we begin to align our thoughts with His perspective.

5. Extend Grace to Yourself

Learning to forgive yourself also means extending the same grace to yourself that you would offer to others. Recognize that you are a work in progress and that God is continually shaping you into the person He has called you to be. Philippians 1:6 reminds us, "*Being confident of this, that He Who began a good work in you will carry it on to completion until the day of Christ Jesus."* Give yourself permission to grow, to make mistakes, and to learn from them.

The Freedom of Self-Forgiveness

Self-forgiveness is not about erasing the past; it is about releasing its hold on your future. It is choosing to live in the light of God's grace rather than the shadow of guilt. It's about learning from past mistakes and move forward. When we forgive ourselves, we open the door to new possibilities, relationships, and opportunities that we were once too burdened to pursue. We allow ourselves to step into the fullness of life that God has for us, a life marked by freedom, peace, and love.

As we move forward in this journey of threefold love, let us embrace the grace that God has lavished upon us. Let us choose to see ourselves not through the lens of our failures, but through the lens of God's redeeming love. In the next part of this book, we will explore what it means to extend this love to others, even in difficult and challenging relationships. But for now, may we take a moment to breathe in the truth that we are forgiven, loved, and free.

PART 3:

EMBRACING OTHERS IN LOVE

Chapter Seven

Loving Your Neighbor as Yourself

D uring college, I had a neighbor who wasn't exactly friendly. In fact, this older lady went out of her way to make things difficult, from loud noises at odd hours to never returning our hellos. For a long time, I avoided her. It was easier to just ignore the situation. But one day, I felt God nudging me to change my approach. Instead of avoiding her, I started looking for little ways to show kindness—offering to take her trash out when I saw her struggling, or simply waving despite the lack of response. Slowly, things changed. She never became my or my roommates' best friend or a great neighbor, but her attitude softened. I learned that loving your neighbor doesn't always mean a grand gesture. Sometimes, it's the consistent choice to show up with grace, even when it's hard.

Loving others is at the heart of the Christian faith. Jesus made it clear that the greatest commandments are to love God and to love our neighbor as ourselves (Matthew 22:37-39). The call to love others is a reflection of God's love working in and through us. However, this commandment is easier said than done. Loving others requires patience, compassion, empathy, and often, a willingness to go beyond our comfort zones.

In this chapter, we will explore what it truly means to love our neighbor as ourselves, examining the depth and scope of this command. We'll delve into practical ways to express this love in our everyday lives and discuss how loving others selflessly transforms our relationships and communities.

Who Is My Neighbor? Expanding Our Understanding of Love

The question, "Who is my neighbor?" was asked of Jesus in Luke 10:29 by a man seeking to define the boundaries of his responsibility to love others. In response, Jesus told the parable of the Good Samaritan. In this story, a man is beaten and left for dead by the side of the road. Both a priest and a Levite, who were religious and respected members of society, pass by without offering help. However, a Samaritan—a person considered an outsider and enemy by Jewish society—stops, cares for the man, and ensures his needs are met.

Through this parable, Jesus challenges the notion that love is confined to those who are like us or within our immediate circle. The Samaritan's act of compassion shows that our "neighbor" is not limited by race, religion, social status, or proximity. Instead, our "neighbor" includes anyone we encounter who is in need of love, mercy, and kindness. Jesus calls us to love expansively, crossing boundaries and setting aside prejudices to reflect the love of God.

This broad definition of "neighbor" requires us to examine our hearts and our attitudes toward others. Are we willing to love those who are different from us? Can we extend kindness to those who may not share our beliefs, political views, values, or way of life? Loving our neighbor as ourselves means that we see the inherent worth in every person, recognizing them as created in the image of God (Genesis 1:27).

Loving Selflessly: The Nature of True Love

True love, as modeled by Jesus, is selfless and sacrificial. In John 15:13, Jesus says, "*Greater love has no one than this: to lay down one's life for one's friends.*" While we may not be called to physically lay down our lives, we are called to put others' needs before our own, to be generous with our time, resources, and compassion. This selflessness is a natural outflow of the love we have received from God. When we grasp how deeply we are loved by Him, we are empowered to love others in the same way.

Selfless love is not about seeking recognition or repayment. In Luke 6:35, Jesus instructs, "*But love your enemies, do good to them, and lend to them without expecting to get anything back.*" This kind of love is radical and counter-cultural. It goes against our natural inclination to protect our own interests or to love only those who love us in return. Yet, it is this selfless, unconditional love that sets us apart as followers of Christ.

In John 13:34-35, Jesus imparts a profound commandment that serves as a cornerstone for Christian living: "*A new command I give you: Love one another. As I have loved you, so you must love one another. By this, everyone will know that you are my disciples if you love one another.*" These verses encapsulate the essence of the threefold love we are called to embrace—love for God, love for self, and love for others. This divine mandate challenges us to elevate our understanding of love beyond mere sentimentality, urging us to engage in a transformative journey that nurtures our spiritual growth and self-discovery.

To love as Jesus loved means to practice an unconditional love that mirrors His grace and compassion. This type of love requires us to recognize that our relationships with others are deeply intertwined with our relationship with God. Each act of love, each moment of kindness, becomes a reflection of our internal state, revealing how we perceive ourselves and our worth in God's eyes. This insight fosters healing in our relationships, as we learn to forgive not only others but ourselves, allowing us to build community rooted in mutual support and understanding.

As we delve deeper into the implications of loving one another, we uncover the beauty of community building. Love manifests most powerfully in the context of relationships; it is in our connections with others that we truly experience God's love. In the body of Christ, every interaction offers an opportunity to demonstrate this love, whether through service, encouragement, or simply being present. When we embody this commandment, we create a vibrant tapestry of faith that invites others into a shared experience of love and belonging. Our communities become places of refuge, where individuals can explore their identities and grow spiritually in an atmosphere of acceptance and grace.

In integrating the teachings of John 13:34-35 into our daily lives, we are invited to reflect on our love languages and how they resonate with both God's love and our relationships with others. By being intentional in our expressions of love, we can create an environment where healing and forgiveness flourish. Each act of love, no matter how small, becomes a testament to our commitment to live out this commandment. As we strive to embody the love of Christ, let us remember that it is through these actions that we not only grow closer to God, but also inspire others to embrace the transformative power of divine love in their own lives.

Practically speaking, loving others selflessly can take many forms. It might mean offering a listening ear to someone who is hurting, forgiving someone who has wronged us, or sacrificing our time to help a friend in need. It can involve giving generously to those who are less fortunate, showing kindness to strangers, or standing up for those who are marginalized. In each of these acts, we reflect the character of God, Who loves us without condition and Who gave His own Son for our sake.

Practicing Empathy and Compassion in Relationships

Empathy and compassion are key components of loving others. Empathy involves putting ourselves in another person's shoes, seeking to understand their feelings, experiences, and perspectives. Compassion goes a step further; it is empathy in action. It compels us to respond to others' needs with kindness and support.

The Bible is filled with examples of Jesus' empathy and compassion. In John 11, we read about Jesus weeping at the death of His friend Lazarus, even though He knew He would raise Lazarus from the dead. Jesus' weeping shows His deep empathy and care for the pain of those around Him. Likewise, we are called to *"rejoice with those who rejoice; mourn with those who mourn"* (Romans 12:15). Loving others means entering into their joys and sorrows, offering them comfort and support.

To practice empathy, we need to be willing to listen to others without judgment or distraction. Often, people don't need us to fix their problems; they simply need to feel heard and understood. Listening with empathy creates a safe space for others to share their struggles and burdens, knowing that they are not alone.

Compassionate love may also involve taking practical steps to help those in need. In James 2:15-16, we are reminded that words alone are not enough: *"Suppose a brother or a sister is without clothes and daily food. If one of you says to them, 'Go in peace; keep warm and well fed,' but does nothing about their physical needs, what good is it?"* True compassion moves us to action, whether it's providing for someone's physical needs, offering a helping hand, or advocating for justice.

Forgiveness: The Ultimate Act of Love

One of the greatest challenges in loving others is extending forgiveness, especially when we have been deeply hurt. Forgiveness is not easy, but it is central to the Christian faith. In Matthew 6:14-15, Jesus teaches, *"For if you forgive other people when they sin against you, your heavenly Father will also forgive you. But if you do not forgive others their sins, your Father will not forgive your sins."* Now, please don't misinterpret this passage! Remember that we have a loving, gracious God. This verse is not meant to be a threat, but rather a reminder of the interconnectedness of forgiveness and love. When we experience God's forgiveness, it enables us to extend that same grace to others.

Forgiveness is not about excusing wrongdoing or forgetting the hurt; it is about releasing the hold that bitterness and resentment have on our hearts. Holding onto unforgiveness only harms us, keeping us trapped in anger and pain. By choosing to forgive, we set ourselves free and open the door for healing and reconciliation.

Loving others through forgiveness may involve praying for those who have wronged us, seeking God's help to release feelings of anger, and, when possible, pursuing reconciliation. Forgiveness is a process, and it may take time to fully let go of the hurt. It is not easy, and often it takes time. However, as we walk this path, we reflect the heart of Christ, Who forgave even those who nailed Him to the cross (Luke 23:34).

Building a Community of Love

The call to love our neighbor extends beyond individual relationships; it encompasses building communities marked by love, compassion, and mutual support. The Early Church in Acts 2:44-47 provides a beautiful example of this kind of community: "*All the believers were together and had everything in common. They sold property and possessions to give to anyone who had need.*" This community of believers shared not only their resources, but also their lives, supporting one another in both spiritual and practical ways.

Today, we are called to be part of a loving community where we can give and receive support. This might be a church, a small group, or a circle of friends who share our faith. In such communities, we find encouragement, accountability, and a space to practice love in tangible ways. Building a community of love requires intentionality—being present for others, serving with a joyful heart, and cultivating an environment where people feel valued and cared for.

Living Out Love in Everyday Life

Loving others as ourselves is not a one-time act; it is a daily choice. It involves small, consistent actions that demonstrate kindness, empathy, and generosity. It means being willing to step out of our comfort zones, to forgive, to listen, and to serve. As we do so, we become conduits of God's love in a world that is desperately in need of hope and healing.

In the next chapter, we will delve into the challenges of loving others, especially in difficult relationships, and explore how God's grace empowers us to extend love even when it seems impossible. For now, may we take a moment to reflect on how we can actively love those around us, embracing the call to be a neighbor to everyone we encounter.

Chapter Eight

Extending Grace in Difficult Relationships

I had a colleague at work who seemed to make everything difficult. No matter what I said or did, they found a way to criticize or complain. It got to the point where I dreaded every interaction with them. One day, after an especially frustrating meeting, I vented to a friend, who asked, 'What if you looked at them with a little more grace?' At first, I was offended. Why should I be the one to extend grace? But later, I realized he was right. Maybe there was more going on in their life than I knew. The next time we interacted, I intentionally shifted my mindset. Instead of reacting, I listened. Slowly, things changed. They didn't magically become easier to work with, but my heart changed. Extending grace became a choice, and that choice brought peace I didn't expect.

Loving others can be one of the most rewarding aspects of life, yet it can also be one of the most challenging, especially when it involves difficult relationships. Whether it's a conflict with a family member, tension with a co-worker, or an encounter with someone who has hurt us deeply, loving others in challenging situations can feel nearly impossible. Yet, this is precisely where Jesus calls us to extend His grace and love in radical ways.

In this chapter, we will explore how to navigate difficult relationships with a spirit of grace and forgiveness. We'll discuss practical ways to love others who are hard to love and how to set healthy boundaries while still showing the love of Christ. By understanding and embracing God's grace in our own lives, we can learn to extend that grace to others, even when it feels most difficult.

The Call to Love Our Enemies

Perhaps one of the most difficult commands that Jesus gave is found in Matthew 5:44: *"But I tell you, love your enemies and pray for those who persecute you."* This radical call to love goes beyond loving those who are kind or likable; it extends to those who may have wronged us, insulted us, or even actively oppose us. Jesus' words challenge our natural inclinations to hold grudges, seek revenge, or avoid those who hurt us.

In this passage, Jesus profoundly challenges the way we typically interact with the world. However, this radical commandment is not merely an ideal, but a pathway to spiritual growth and self-discovery. By embodying this teaching, we can cultivate a deeper connection with God, ourselves, and others, transforming our hearts in ways that reflect divine love. Embracing such a mindset invites us to engage in mindfulness, nurturing compassion for those who may not understand our journey or who may even oppose it.

When we examine the essence of loving our enemies, it becomes clear that this love is not about condoning harmful behavior or relinquishing our boundaries. Instead, it is an invitation to rise above resentment and anger, choosing forgiveness as a means of healing our hearts. In the context of interpersonal relationships, this teaching encourages us to reflect on our emotional responses and the narratives we create around those who hurt us. By practicing self-compassion and understanding our own vulnerabilities, we can begin to see our adversaries not just as opponents but as fellow travelers on the path of life, each wrestling with their own burdens.

Integrating this principle into our daily lives requires a commitment to prayer and reflection. Pray for those who challenge us, not merely as a formality, but as a sacred practice that softens our hearts and opens our minds. This act of prayer can serve as a powerful tool for spiritual growth, allowing us to recognize and honor our feelings while simultaneously fostering a sense of connection with others. As we engage in this spiritual practice, we cultivate a deeper understanding of grace and forgiveness, essential components in healing relationships and building a faith-based community grounded in love.

Embracing the command to love our enemies can be transformative. It encourages us to step back from our ego and to seek the divine perspective in conflicts. When we view others through the lens of love, we create space for understanding and empathy, essential elements in nurturing healthy relationships. This transformative love is not limited to our friends and family, but extends to everyone we encounter, reminding us that we are all reflections of God's image.

The practice of loving our enemies is a call to action that resonates deeply within the threefold love framework: love for God, self, and others. It challenges us to reflect on how we embody this divine love in every interaction, fostering a spirit of compassion that transcends differences. As we strive to integrate these spiritual practices into our daily lives, let us embrace the beauty of this commandment, allowing it to guide us on our journey of faith and connection. In doing so, we not only honor our relationship with God but also enrich our lives and the lives of those around us, creating a ripple effect of love that touches the world.

And again, the call to love our enemies is not about condoning their behavior or pretending that everything is okay. It is about choosing to respond to hostility with grace and compassion rather than bitterness and hatred, because we recognize that we've been extended that grace as well. Yes, I know! This is difficult. Easier said than done, right? And yet, in Romans 12:20-21, Paul writes, *"If your enemy is hungry, feed him; if he is thirsty, give him something to drink... Do not be overcome by evil, but overcome evil with good."* This passage highlights the power of love to transform even the most difficult relationships. When we choose to love our enemies, we reflect the heart of God, Who *"causes His sun to rise on the evil and the good"* (Matthew 5:45).

Loving our enemies is not something we can do in our own strength; it requires the work of the Holy Spirit within us. It involves praying for those who have hurt us, asking God to change our hearts first, and then seeking His help to see them through His eyes. As we pray for our enemies, we begin to release the hold that anger and resentment have on us, allowing God's grace to flow through us.

Practicing Forgiveness in Difficult Relationships

Forgiveness is at the core of extending grace in difficult relationships. When we have been hurt or betrayed, the idea of forgiveness can feel like letting someone off the hook for their wrongdoing. However, forgiveness is not about excusing bad behavior; it is about freeing ourselves from the chains of bitterness that keep us bound.

Jesus' teaching on forgiveness is clear and uncompromising. In Matthew 18:21-22, Peter asks Jesus how many times he should forgive someone who sins against him, suggesting up to seven times. Jesus replies, *"I tell you, not seven times, but seventy-seven times."* This response emphasizes that forgiveness is not a one-time act, but actually an ongoing practice. It is a choice we must make repeatedly, every time the pain resurfaces or the offense comes to mind.

Again, I want to re-emphasize... forgiveness does not mean that we forget what happened or that we allow others to continue to hurt us. Instead, it means releasing our right to seek revenge or harbor resentment. It means entrusting the situation to God, Who is the ultimate judge, and choosing to move forward in freedom—whether justice is served or not. When we forgive, we break the cycle of hurt and open the door for healing, both in our own hearts and in the relationship.

Practical ways to practice forgiveness include:

- Praying for the person: This shifts our focus from our pain to God's love and allows Him to work in our hearts.

- Choosing not to dwell on the offense: When thoughts of the hurt arise, remind yourself of your decision to forgive and ask God to help you release it.

- Seeking peace, not necessarily reconciliation: Forgiveness does not always result in reconciliation, especially if the other person is not willing to change. It is possible to forgive and let go without resuming a close relationship—or even a relationship at all.

Setting Healthy Boundaries While Loving Others

Loving others does not mean allowing ourselves to be mistreated or taken advantage of. There is a difference between loving someone and enabling harmful behavior. Boundaries are essential in difficult relationships, as they protect our well-being and help us maintain a healthy balance between grace and self-respect.

As we learned before, Jesus Himself set boundaries during His ministry. In Mark 1:35-38, after spending time in solitude and prayer, Jesus chose to leave a crowd of people who were seeking more of His miracles to continue His mission in other towns. He was not driven by others' demands, but by the purpose that the Father had given Him. Similarly, we must discern when to say no, when to step back, and when to protect our emotional, mental, and spiritual health.

Setting boundaries in difficult relationships can include:

- Limiting contact: If a relationship is toxic or abusive, it may be necessary to limit or even cut off contact for your well-being.

- Communicating your needs: Express your feelings and needs clearly and respectfully. For example, let the other person know what behaviors are hurtful to you and what changes, if any, you may need to maintain a positive relationship. Keep in mind, however, that they may need the same coming from you.

- Seeking support: Talk to trusted friends, mentors, or counselors for guidance on navigating complex relationships. They can provide perspective and help you establish healthy boundaries.

Boundaries are not about punishing the other person; they are about creating a space where love can be given and received in a healthy way. By setting boundaries, we honor both ourselves and the other person, allowing room for growth, respect, and genuine connection.

Loving Through the Power of Grace

In difficult relationships, extending love requires us to draw upon the grace we have received from God. Grace is undeserved favor, and it is at the heart of the Gospel. We are called to love others not because they deserve it, but because we have been loved by God even when we were undeserving. Colossians 3:13 instructs us, *"Bear with each other and forgive one another if any of you has a grievance against someone. Forgive as the Lord forgave you."*

This call to action is deeply rooted in the understanding that just as the Lord has forgiven us, we too must extend that mercy to others. In a world filled with misunderstandings and conflicts, embracing this divine principle can transform our interpersonal relationships, fostering an environment of compassion, empathy, and love.

Forgiveness is not merely an act; it is a way of being that nurtures our spiritual growth and self-discovery. When we choose to forgive, we release the burdens of resentment and anger that weigh heavily on our hearts. This liberation opens the door for deeper connections with ourselves and others. It invites us to engage in mindfulness, reflecting on our own shortcomings while recognizing the humanity in those around us. In this space of understanding, we cultivate self-compassion, allowing ourselves and others the grace to make mistakes and learn from them.

The power of forgiveness extends beyond individual relationships; it is a vital component of building a faith-based community. When we embody the spirit of forgiveness through loving grace, we create a culture of acceptance and healing. This atmosphere encourages open communication, where individuals feel safe to express their vulnerabilities and seek reconciliation. By actively practicing forgiveness, we demonstrate the love of Christ in our interactions, reinforcing the bonds that unite us as a community dedicated to spiritual growth and mutual support.

As we integrate the teachings of this verse into our daily lives, we find that forgiveness becomes a transformative practice. It is an act of surrender, a conscious choice to prioritize love over bitterness. In doing so, we align ourselves with God's heart, allowing His grace to flow through us. This alignment nurtures our personal well-being and enables us to respond with kindness and understanding in challenging situations. Through this lens, we see forgiveness not as a weakness, but as a profound strength that enriches our relationships. Each act of forgiveness becomes a step towards greater unity, healing, and love, reinforcing the essence of our Christian calling to live in harmony with one another.

When we remember the grace that God has shown us, we are empowered to extend that grace to others. This does not mean ignoring wrongs or allowing harmful behavior to continue; it means choosing to respond with kindness, patience, and love, even in the face of difficulty. It means recognizing that every person, no matter how challenging, is loved by God and is worthy of our compassion.

Releasing Outcomes to God

One of the hardest aspects of loving others in difficult relationships is releasing the outcome to God. We cannot control how others will respond to our love, forgiveness, or boundaries. Some relationships may heal and grow stronger, while others may remain strained or even come to an end. Ultimately, however, our role is still to love faithfully, showing grace and kindness, while trusting God with the results, no matter what happens.

Proverbs 3:5-6 encourages us to "*Trust in the Lord with all your heart and lean not on your own understanding; in all your ways submit to Him, and He will make your paths straight.*" Loving others, especially in difficult circumstances, is an act of submission to God. We place our hope, our pain, and our desire for reconciliation in His hands, knowing that He is able to work in ways we cannot see.

Loving others in difficult relationships is not easy, but it brings a profound freedom. It frees us from the bondage of bitterness, resentment, and anger. It allows us to experience the depth of God's love as we reflect it to others. And it transforms our hearts, making us more like Christ, Who loved us while we were still sinners (Romans 5:8).

In the final chapter of this book, we will explore how building a community of love can strengthen our ability to live out this call to love others, even when it is challenging. For now, may we take a moment to pray for those relationships that test our capacity to love, asking God to fill us with His grace and to guide us in extending love, even when it feels impossible.

Chapter Nine

Building a Loving Community

A few years ago, I moved to a new city. This also meant attending a new church. At first, everything felt distant and disconnected, much different than what I was used to. People were nice, but mostly kept to themselves, and there wasn't much interaction beyond a polite wave. I knew that I wanted to change that—at least in a small way. So, my wife and I decided to organize a simple get-together at our place. We invited some young families with kids similar in age as ours and hoped for the best. The day of the get-together, we were nervous. What if no one showed up? But slowly, one by one, families began to trickle in. By the end of the evening, we had kids playing together, adults chatting like old friends, and an overwhelming sense of connection. It wasn't a grand gesture, but it was a reminder that community is built on small, intentional actions. That get-together became a constant event. Building a loving community doesn't require big events—it just requires a willingness to bring people together.

Loving others is not meant to be a solitary endeavor; it flourishes in the context of community. From the earliest days of creation, God acknowledged that "*It is not good for the man to be alone*" (Genesis 2:18). We are designed for relationships, for connection with others who support, encourage, and challenge us to grow in love. The Christian faith, at its core, is communal. The church is often referred to as the "*body of Christ*," each member interdependent and vital to the whole (1 Corinthians 12:12-27).

In this chapter, we will explore what it means to build a loving community and how it plays a crucial role in our spiritual growth. We'll discuss the characteristics of a Christ-centered community, practical ways to cultivate a community of love, and how being part of such a community strengthens our ability to live out the threefold love of God, self, and others.

The Importance of Community in the Christian Faith

Throughout the Bible, we see that God places a high value on community. The Early Church, as described in Acts 2:42-47, provides a beautiful example of this: " *They devoted themselves to the apostles' teaching and to fellowship, to the breaking of bread and to prayer... All the believers were together and had everything in common.*" This passage depicts a community where love was not just a sentiment, but a way of life. The believers shared not only their resources, but also their lives. They prayed together, ate together, and supported each other's needs.

Being part of a loving community is vital for our spiritual well-being. In a world where individualism is often emphasized, it can be easy to overlook the importance of fellowship. Yet, it is within the context of community that we learn to live out the command to love our neighbor as ourselves. In community, we are challenged to forgive, to serve, and to give generously. We are reminded that our faith is not just about our personal relationship with God, but also about how we interact with those around us.

In Hebrews 10:24-25, we are called to consider how we can spur one another on toward love and good deeds. The author writes, *"Let us consider how we can stir up one another to love and good works. Let us not neglect our meeting together, as some people do, but encourage one another, especially now that the day of His return is drawing near."* This passage serves as a potent reminder of the interconnectedness of our faith and our relationships with one another. The act of encouraging and supporting each other in our spiritual journeys is not merely an option; it is a divine command that fosters a loving community. When we gather together, whether in worship, study, play, or fellowship, we create an environment where love flourishes, filling our hearts and extending to those around us. This intentional connection is essential, especially in this world that often promotes isolation and individualism.

As we engage with others, we must remember that our actions and words carry weight. The encouragement we offer can ignite a spark of hope in someone struggling, reminding them of their worth and the love God has for them. When we genuinely love God, we begin to see ourselves through His eyes, recognizing our intrinsic value. This self-acceptance empowers us to love others authentically, creating a ripple effect of compassion and understanding within our communities.

The call to not give up meeting together resonates deeply in our fast-paced, often disconnected society. When we prioritize gathering with fellow believers, we enhance our spiritual growth and reinforce our collective identity as children of God. These moments of fellowship provide opportunities for mindful reflection, allowing us to share our struggles and triumphs in a supportive environment. By cultivating this sense of belonging, we create sacred spaces where healing can occur, and forgiveness can take root, transforming our interpersonal relationships into mirrors of divine love.

Hebrews 10:24-25 reminds us that our faith is not a solitary endeavor. It is a collective experience that thrives on connection, encouragement, and love. As we commit to fostering a community rooted in these principles, we reflect the heart of God to the world around us. In doing so, we cultivate a divine connection that nurtures us, enriches our relationships, and empowers us to live out our faith with authenticity and joy. Let us embrace the beauty of loving God, ourselves, and others, for in this triad lies the essence of our spiritual growth and fulfillment.

Honoring One Another In Community

In Romans 12:10, we are called to *"Be devoted to one another in love. Honor one another above yourselves."* This simple, yet profound directive encapsulates the essence of the threefold love that we are encouraged to embrace: love for God, love for ourselves, and love for others. The beauty of this verse lies in its challenge to prioritize the needs and well-being of others, which not only reflects our faith, but also nurtures our spiritual growth. As we seek to deepen our relationship with God, we must remember that our devotion to one another is a direct expression of our love for Him, creating a divine connection that enriches our lives and the lives of those around us.

Devotion in relationships requires mindfulness and self-compassion. When we honor one another above ourselves, we cultivate an environment where love can flourish. This means actively listening to others, being present in conversations, and showing empathy in our interactions. It is in these moments of connection that we discover the power of love, allowing us to communicate affection in ways that resonate deeply with others. By understanding and applying the principles, we can create more meaningful relationships that reflect the love of Christ, fostering a community rooted in mutual respect and care.

In our journey of self-discovery, we often grapple with the question of our worthiness. However, Romans 12:10 reminds us that honoring others does not diminish our value; instead, it elevates our understanding of love and community. By embracing our identity as beloved children of God, we can approach our relationships with a sense of abundance rather than scarcity. This perspective allows us to extend grace and forgiveness, healing wounds and fostering reconciliation in our interactions. As we practice this divine love, we become conduits of God's grace, transforming our communities into spaces of hope and healing.

Building a faith-based community that embodies the principles of honoring each other requires intentionality and commitment. We must strive to reflect the love we receive from God by nurturing relationships that are characterized by support, encouragement, and accountability. When we come together in love, we create a powerful force for change, inspiring one another to live out our faith in tangible ways that impact our communities and beyond.

By devoting ourselves to one another, we embody the heart of Christ and cultivate a transformative love that transcends barriers and differences. As we embrace this threefold love, we not only grow spiritually, but also enrich our lives and the lives of those around us. In doing so, we fulfill our divine calling to be reflections of God's love in a world that desperately needs it. Let us commit to living out this commandment, honoring and uplifting one another in community as we embark on this journey of faith together.

Characteristics of a Loving Community

In 1 Corinthians 16:14, the Apostle Paul provides a simple yet profound directive: *"Let all that you do be done in love."* This exhortation invites us to reflect deeply on the nature of love as it permeates our lives and interactions. As we embark on our journey of spiritual growth and self-discovery, it is essential to recognize that love is not merely an emotion; it is a powerful force that shapes our actions, influences our relationships, and ultimately defines our connection with God, ourselves, and others. When we allow love to guide our decisions and behaviors, we cultivate an environment where authentic relationships can thrive.

Embracing the threefold love—loving God, loving ourselves, and loving others—becomes a transformative practice that impacts every aspect of our being. Love for God anchors us in faith and inspires a commitment to spiritual disciplines that deepen our relationship with the divine. When we genuinely love ourselves, we acknowledge our worth as creations of God, allowing us to practice self-compassion and mindfulness. This self-love becomes the foundation from which we extend love to others, fostering connection and understanding in our interpersonal relationships. Each expression of love, whether in thought, word, or deed, resonates with the divine purpose that unites us.

In the context of community, Paul's reminder to act in love challenges us to foster faith-based connections that uplift and empower one another. When we prioritize love in our interactions, we create a culture of acceptance and support within our communities. Practicing love means being present in the moment, recognizing the significance of each interaction, and choosing responses that reflect compassion and grace. As we navigate life's challenges and joys, the principle of doing everything in love serves as a guiding light. It encourages us to pause, reflect, and choose love, even in the face of difficulty.

The call to let all that we do be done in love is an invitation to fully embrace the divine connection that exists within us and among us. As we cultivate this love, we experience profound personal growth and foster meaningful connections that enrich our lives. A Christ-centered, loving community is characterized by several key qualities that reflect the heart of God. Here are a few of the most important characteristics:

1. Acceptance and Grace

A loving community is one where people are accepted just as they are, without judgment or condemnation. This acceptance is rooted in the grace of God, Who welcomes each of us with open arms despite our flaws and failures. In Romans 15:7, Paul encourages believers to *"Accept one another, then, just as Christ accepted you, in order to bring praise to God."* When we extend this grace to others, we create a safe environment where people can be authentic, share their struggles, and experience the healing power of love.

2. Encouragement and Support

Life is full of challenges, and we need others to walk alongside us, offering encouragement and support. In 1 Thessalonians 5:11, we are urged to *"encourage one another and build each other up."* A loving community is one where people are uplifted, where successes are celebrated, and where those who are struggling are not left to face their difficulties alone.

It's a place where words of affirmation, prayers, and acts of kindness flow freely, reminding us that we are not on this journey by ourselves.

3. Mutual Service and Generosity

Jesus modeled a life of service, and He calls us to do the same. A loving community is marked by mutual service, where members use their gifts and resources to meet each other's needs. In Galatians 5:13, Paul writes, *"Serve one another humbly in love."* This kind of service is not about obligation or seeking recognition; it is about love in action. It includes helping those in need, giving generously, and being willing to lay down our time and energy for the sake of others.

4. Truth and Accountability

Love involves speaking the truth, even when it is difficult. A loving community is not just about affirming one another; it is also about holding each other accountable in love. Ephesians 4:15 calls us to *"speak the truth in love,"* helping one another grow and mature in faith. In such a community, people are encouraged to pursue holiness and to live lives that honor God, with the understanding that accountability is not condemnation, but an expression of love and care.

Cultivating a Loving Community

Building a loving community requires intentionality and effort. It does not happen overnight, but through consistent acts of love, kindness, and humility. Here are some practical ways to cultivate a community that reflects the love of Christ:

1. Be Present and Invest Time

True community is built on relationships, and relationships require time and presence. Make an effort to be involved in the lives of others. This might mean joining a small group, attending church gatherings, or simply reaching out to people for a meal and conversation. By investing time in others, we show that they are valued and that we are committed to walking alongside them in both good times and bad.

2. Practice Vulnerability

A loving community is one where people can be honest and open about their struggles, fears, and doubts. Practicing vulnerability involves being willing to share your own experiences and to listen with empathy when others share theirs. Vulnerability fosters deep, authentic relationships, allowing people to connect on a heart level. It also creates an atmosphere where grace can be experienced as we support and pray for each other.

3. Serve and Encourage

Look for ways to serve those in your community. It could be through simple acts like offering a meal to someone going through a difficult time, helping a friend move, serving and getting involved at church, or even volunteering at church community events. Acts of service demonstrate love in practical ways and strengthen the bonds of community. Additionally, make it a habit to encourage others. A kind word, a thoughtful note, or a prayer of support can make a profound difference in someone's life.

4. Create Space for Fellowship

Fellowship is about more than just attending church services; it's about sharing life together. Create opportunities for fellowship by hosting gatherings, sharing meals, or organizing activities that bring people together. These shared experiences build trust, joy, and a sense of belonging, which are essential for a thriving community.

Strengthening Your Love Through Community

Being part of a loving community not only blesses others, but also strengthens your own ability to love. In community, we learn patience, forgiveness, and humility as we navigate relationships with people who are different from us. We are reminded that love is not just a feeling, but a series of intentional choices to serve, support, and encourage one another.

A loving community provides the support we need to keep growing in our relationship with God. When we are surrounded by others who share our faith, we are encouraged to pursue spiritual disciplines, to seek God in times of difficulty, and to celebrate His goodness. The love that we receive and give from and to our community equips us to better love ourselves and to extend that love to the world around us.

A Reflection of God's Kingdom

Ultimately, a loving community is a reflection of God's Kingdom on Earth. As we read earlier, Jesus said, *"By this everyone will know that you are my disciples, if you love one another"* (John 13:35). The way we love each other in community is a powerful testimony to the world of God's transforming love. It is through our unity, service, and generosity that people see glimpses of God's grace and are drawn to Him.

As we conclude this journey through the threefold love of God, self, and others, let us commit to building communities of love that embody the heart of Christ. May we be known for our acceptance, encouragement, generosity, and truth. And may we continually grow in our love for God, ourselves, and each other, knowing that this is the life to which we are called.

In the final chapter, we will bring together all that we have explored in this book and reflect on what it means to live a life of love in our everyday walk. For now, may we take a moment to thank God for the communities He has placed us in and seek ways to contribute to building them up in love.

Chapter Ten

Conclusion: Living a Life of Threefold Love

I used to think that loving God, myself, and others were three separate tasks—almost like a checklist to get through. But over time, I've learned they're deeply interconnected. I remember one day, sitting by the lake, watching my then much younger kids play, and feeling this overwhelming sense of gratitude. It wasn't because everything in life was perfect—it wasn't. But in that moment, I realized that my love for God was shaping the way I loved myself, and in turn, it was shaping the way I was loving my family. It was a quiet, peaceful realization, but it was profound. Living out this threefold love isn't about perfection; it's about continually showing up—being present with God, being kind to myself, and sharing that love with others. It's a journey, and I'm still learning every day.

As we bring this journey to a close, let's reflect on the beautiful, interconnected nature of the threefold love we've explored. This journey began with understanding the essence of God's unconditional love. We moved on to embracing self-love through the lens of how God views us, and we concluded with the call to extend this love to others—even when it is challenging. At its core, this threefold love is not just a set of ideals; it's a way of life, a reflection of our faith, and a testament to the transformative power of God's love.

The greatest commandment Jesus gave us is to *"love the Lord your God with all your heart and with all your soul and with all your mind"* and to *"love your neighbor as yourself"* (Matthew 22:37-39). These words are the foundation of a fulfilling Christian life. When we make loving God our primary focus, we begin to see ourselves and others through His eyes. This love reshapes our attitudes, our relationships, and our actions. It leads us to become people who live out the Gospel in every interaction, every act of service, and every step of our daily walk.

Putting Love into Practice

The call to live a life of threefold love is not about achieving perfection. It's about making daily choices to align our hearts with God's love and to extend that love to others and ourselves. It's about inviting God's presence into every aspect of our lives, allowing His love to transform how we think, speak, and act. Here are a few practical ways to continue putting this love into practice:

1. Cultivate Your Relationship with God: Make time daily to connect with God, whether through prayer, worship, and/or reading His Word. Loving God with all your heart, soul, and mind starts with seeking His presence and listening to His voice. The more you experience His love, the more you will be empowered to love yourself and others.

2. Practice Self-Compassion: Remember that loving yourself is not about being self-centered; it's about accepting who you are in Christ. Embrace self-care, extend grace to yourself when you make mistakes, and let go of guilt and self-condemnation. As you grow in self-love, you will be more equipped to show love and compassion to others.

3. Serve and Love Others Intentionally: Look for ways to serve and encourage those around you. Whether it's through small acts of kindness, offering a listening ear, or forgiving those who have hurt you, let your actions reflect the love of Christ. Seek to build and nurture a community where love, grace, and support are freely given.

4. Pray for Difficult Relationships: Loving others includes extending grace to those who are hard to love. Pray for those who challenge you, and ask God to give you the strength to forgive, set boundaries, and show kindness. Trust that God is working in your heart and in the lives of those you are called to love.

A Daily Commitment to Love

Living a life of love is an ongoing process. There will be days when it comes easily and days when it feels like an uphill battle. In those moments, remember that you are not walking this path alone. God's love is the source and sustainer of your ability to love. When you feel weary, draw near to Him, and allow His love to fill and refresh you.

The threefold love—loving God, loving yourself, and loving others—is like a cycle that continuously feeds into itself. The more you love God, the more you understand your worth and value in His eyes, which then frees you to love others without reservation. Likewise, as you love others, you find deeper joy and fulfillment, drawing you closer to God and reinforcing your self-worth. It is a dynamic, life-giving process that grows and deepens over time.

A Light to the World

When we live out this threefold love, we become a light in a world that is often marked by division, hatred, and self-centeredness. Our love becomes a powerful testimony of God's presence in our lives (John 13:35). It is through love that we make His grace, mercy, and compassion visible to the world around us.

Imagine the impact if each of us committed to living this life of love in our homes, workplaces, communities, and churches. How might our relationships be transformed? How might our communities change? The world is in desperate need of love—the kind of love that reflects God's heart and brings hope, healing, forgiveness, transformation, and reconciliation. This is the love that we are called to embody.

A Lifelong Journey

As we close this book, let's remember that the journey of threefold love is not about arriving at a final destination, but about growing deeper in love each day. It's a journey that requires grace, patience, and dependence on God. There will be challenges along the way, but there will also be moments of profound joy and transformation as you live out the love that you have received.

May this journey of threefold love inspire you to draw closer to God, to embrace yourself as He sees you, and to extend His love to everyone you encounter. And may you find that in giving and receiving love, you experience the fullness of life that God has created you for.

Now, go forth, living lives marked by the love that comes from God, overflows to ourselves, and touches the lives of others. This is the essence of the threefold love—a love that changes hearts, transforms communities, and ultimately brings glory to God.

Acknowledgements

Writing *Threefold Love* has been a journey of deep reflection, growth, and gratitude. It would not have been possible without the incredible people who have shaped me along the way.

To my parents, whose love and support have been a constant source of strength—thank you for raising me with values that have shaped the man I am today. Your unwavering belief in me and the foundation you provided is something I carry with me in every chapter of my life.

To the pastors and mentors who have inspired me—your wisdom, guidance, and example have profoundly influenced my spiritual walk. Thank you for being a beacon of faith, helping me navigate life's complexities, and challenging me to seek truth and love in all I do.

To my teachers and professors, who taught me not just about academics, but about life, God, and everything in between—thank you for your patience, your lessons, and for encouraging me to ask the big questions. You have broadened my perspective and nurtured my curiosity, and for that, I am forever grateful.

Each of you has played a vital role in the creation of this book. *Threefold Love* is not just my work—it is a testament to the community of support that has shaped me. I am deeply thankful for all you've done. This one is for all of you.

About the Author

O bed Olivarría was born in Mexicali, Mexico and spent his youth as a fully bicultural transnational citizen. He has a passion for writing both fiction and nonfiction, public speaking, composing, arranging, and performing mostly jazz music, as well as traveling around the world. He loves the thrill of adrenaline-pumping activities, but also the quiet reflection he gets from writing and creating.

Obed has worked as a youth and young adult pastor, as a freelance graphic designer, as a session musician, as a ministry consultant, and as university dean. Having worked at every level of the education system, from pre-k to university, has given him an expedition to the human psyche. He has a dynamic love of life and ministry, and he is a deep thinker, and an honest intellectual to the Gospel of Jesus.

Obed lives in sunny Orange County, California with his charming wife and two energetic children, where he works as a school psychologist by day. In the future, Obed hopes to be able to continue to write inspiring books that entertain, but also challenge the status quo. On a personal level, he would like to visit every country in the world, perhaps drawing inspiration from these travels for another great story.

www.ingramcontent.com/pod-product-compliance
Lightning Source LLC
Chambersburg PA
CBHW070449130626
46553CB00006B/2325